Working Lives

Memoirs of Rural Ireland

Published By
As Dúchas Dóchas

Edited by

David O'Grady

Published in Ireland in 2001 by
As Dúchas Dóchas,
Old County Council Offices,
Bishop Street,
Newcastle West,
Co. Limerick,
Ireland.
Tel: +353 (0)69 62215
Web: http://www.asduchasdochas.pro.ie
E-mail: asduchasdochas@eircom.net

Editor/ Project Manager
David O'Grady

Proof Reading/ Assistant Project Manager
Catherine Hartigan

Cover Design and Layout
John Kavanagh and David O'Grady

The following have worked at As Dúchas Dóchas
and have contributed to this publication:
Siobhan Conaghan, Eilish Creedon, Elaine Cronin, Kerry Cummins, Valerie Cunningham, Anne Dowling, Susanne Ford, Louise Hartnett, Esther Horgan, Sandra Hurley, Ellen Lisa Joyce, Tanya Joyce, John Kavanagh, Caroline Kearns, Helen Kennelly, Shane Lynch, Louise McCarthy, Finola McCrann, Niamh McDonald, Ruth McParland, Mairéad Noonan, Eilish O'Flaherty, Mary Reidy, Mary Roche, Loretta Ryder, Karen Sheehan, Joseph Sillery, Susan Sparling and Martina Woulfe.

ISBN: 0-9541802-1-6

Front Cover Photo: Patie Meade's forge, Abbeyfeale, Co. Limerick c. 1960.
Back Cover Photo: Dowling Family, Ardagh.

You board the train of life to go on your worldly ride
And day by day you travel until the tracks they will divide.
The early years of travel are a sort of guiding tour
But after childhood you must choose the paths that you will endure.
The lonely or the selfless track, the good or evil train,
And as you choose so well, you loose or you will truly gain.
So buy your ticket cautiously, be careful of each stop
And do not let the luggage of your virtues ever drop.
Remember, that your train of life must go along its track -
You make the final choice...there is no turning back.

Patrick Fitzsimons
Shanagolden
2001

Contents

Foreword

Cathaoirleach of Limerick County Council

I am delighted that Limerick Council is actively involved in this publication and with the As Dúchas Dóchas project. Working Lives gathers a moving and reminiscent selection of interviews and articulations from the people of West Limerick and presents an opportunity to people both living in and outside the county to experience the rich tradition evident in this area.

The work represents the various themes in our society and culture, both spiritual and temporal, including the early life and school, the working life and politics, the supernatural and folklore, religious matters and love. It not only gives one a sense of place but also a sense of the self-worth and diversity in County Limerick. The various life stories in this publication will enchant and fascinate the reader, helping to embody the county and demonstrate the value of collecting information on the more transient heritage that all too often fades quickly over generations.

I would like to compliment everyone involved in the As Dúchas Dóchas project and wish them continued success in the future. This book is very much a community based project and the company must be congratulated on commissioning this work. Their growth from a small beginning to a publishing establishment is a notable achievement and their ability to help young people to enter the workforce is commendable.

Michael Brennan

Chairman of As Dúchas Dóchas

Working Lives initiates the publication programme for As Dúchas Dóchas, the Newcastle West based Local Training Initiative Project, and signals another success for FÁS as our partner and we are grateful for their constant help and support. I would like to thank Catherine Hurley, Senior Development Officer, for her vision in making this project a reality.

This very effective partnership has already produced valuable research to strengthen the work of As Dúchas Dóchas as a research project and this publication represents a further step in showing the importance of local history and is an indication of the positive role that projects like this one can achieve in their areas.

David O'Grady, Project Manager of As Dúchas Dóchas, was given control of the compilation of the material and I thank him for his devotion and enthusiasm for the project. The direction that both he and Catherine Murphy, Assistant Project Manager, have shown has been exceptional and the many people who have left to take up employment or to return to further education can be proud of the contribution they have made to this book.

I would like to extend a special word of thanks to County Manager Pat O'Connor, retired Bainisteoir Chontae Riobéard Ó Ceallaigh, and Board Members of As Dúchas Dóchas - Gerry Behan, Oliver Killeen, Catherine Hurley, Helen Walsh, Paul Foley and Aileen Dillane - for their valued support since the project began. They have given us a vote of confidence in our undertakings and I am confident that this will be further rewarded in due course.

Damien Brady

Introduction

Folklore, the study of the folk-mind and the investigation of the world and ways of ordinary people, continues to fascinate, with the culture of the ordinary citizen and the traditions of the past remaining very significant. Taking this into consideration, As Dúchas Dóchas staff set out in the fall of 2000 and began the process of interviewing people in the West County Limerick on their working lives. Our selection was, more or less, from the people living in the county west of a line from Askeaton to Dromcolliher, an area teeming with local history and folklore ranging from the most unassuming ring fort or standing stone to the commanding structure of a castle in the countryside.

In the past year, we have met people from all walks of life in the area, from blacksmiths, shoemakers and stonemasons to former soldiers, farmers and dancehall owners. Their stories have been frank and intimate, detailing all aspects of their lives from the earliest memory to the present day and all in between that has made them who they are. Each one of their accounts represents Ireland, past and present.

In carrying out a project such as this, we were encouraged by such work as that done by the Irish Folklore Commission in their School's Scheme. In the 1930's, or "De Valera's Ireland", there was a sense that so much heritage and tradition had already been lost and the lack of any documentary evidence of what had been retained had to be remedied. The appeal was based on the grounds that the "story of the Irish countryman will never be known" unless the real tradition and folklore was recorded in every townland throughout the country.

In 1935, the government set up the Irish Folklore Commission with the primary job of collecting material. For such a task it is obvious that planning and method were very important, especially if the material was ever to be classified and made available to students. With the help of the Department of Education in 1937-38, The Schools' Scheme collection of folklore was initiated by the Commission throughout the National Schools of the 26 counties. It was carried out by school children, aged 11-14, who followed specially prepared guidelines. The net result was that 4,574 official notebooks were returned to the Commission and these have continued to be used by students of social history both here and in Europe.

This experiment in collecting folklore was unique and has not been repeated on a national scale but we initiated it in a small way here in west Limerick with those who hold that last link to that era in Irish history. These compelling life stories detail part of what has made Ireland what it is today, the evolution of the country from a dominion and colony to a proud, distinguished and prosperous nation.

A special thanks goes to all the contributors to this volume of work, both interviewees and collectors, to whom the book belongs. The experience had by both was, I hope, rewarding and beneficial. Go maire sibh go léir an céad. Also, special thanks goes to staff of the Limerick County Library Service, FÁS, Limerick County Council, St. Anne's Nursing Home, The Tall Trees Nursing Home, Cahermoyle Nursing Home and the many people who offered their humour and hospitality to us throughout the past year or so.

The nature of oral folklore can cause it to die out from generation to generation and therefore, it is important that it is recorded for posterity and shared among the community from which it evolved. Moreover, each person in his or her own way has a duty to the individual who is brimming of information that has not yet been collected. That person may well have passed on before any effort is made to collect material from them and this will be to the detriment of society and history in general.

To quote the historian Francis Shaw - writing in the 1940's, just after the publication of Sean O'Suilleabháin's "Handbook of Irish Folklore" - "When truth and beauty and goodness cannot be found in modern civilisation, we are forced to seek for those values in other places... we must retrace our steps to where we strayed from the road."

David O'Grady
Editor
October 2001

Buíochas Speisialta

To all the interviewees and their families which took part in this project
Matrons, managemaent and staff at Cahermoyle Nursing Home, Ardagh,
Saint Anne's Nursing Home, Dromcolliher and
Tall Tree's Nursing Home, Askeaton.
The Board members of As Dúchas Dóchas
Aileen Dillane and County Library Staff, Newcastle West.
Damien Brady and County Library Headquarters Staff, Limerick.
Catherine Hurley and colleagues, FÁS, Newcastle West and Limerick.
Limerick County Council, Newcastle West and Limerick.
David Ward and Co., Accounts, Abbeyfeale.

Families and friends of As Dúchas Dóchas staff
for their encouragement and support.

Bill Cahill and Mick McCormack

Interviewer: Could you state your names and addresses?

Bill Cahill: Bill Cahill, Moneymohill, Ballyhahill, Co. Limerick.

Mick McCormack: Michael McCormack, Ballycarney, Clarina, Co. Limerick.

Interviewer: Bill, was there many of you in your family?

Bill: There was fifteen in my family but two died when they were young, one of them with leukaemia and the other with some other incurable disease, and the rest survived. Today, there are eight or nine of them in America and the rest of them are in this country.

Interviewer: And Mick, was there many in your family?

Mick: There were four boys and two girls and are all dead now except for one brother alive in County Clare.

Interviewer: You come from a farming background Bill. Did your mother and father work in the farming business? Did your mother ever work outside the farm?

Bill: No, it was the way my father married into the place.

Interviewer: Did you keep on the same farm?

Bill: Yeah, I did but you can't farm now, it just doesn't pay. It doesn't pay to leave any kind of a job now. I went into farming in a small kind of a way with twelve or fourteen cows, whatever we used to have. We had close to twenty-one one time before my brother died but we went out of that then going for suckling. The health gave way then and it had to go as well.

Interviewer: Did you find a change from when you were young and took over the farm first to farming in later years?

Bill: Oh yes, going out of the hay of course was a big change. I saved hay always but almost everybody else were going out with the silage and then of course the weather these late years put them out of the hay business anyway. There is no weather now that would save hay.

Interviewer: Where did your parents work Mick?

Mick: Well, my mother was always doing the housework at home and there would be a few pigs and fowl kept in the place and that sort of thing which she would be working at also. She would be doing her own bit, selling the eggs and that sort of thing. My father then was working outside on farms with farmers.

Interviewer: Where did you go to school and what were those days like?

Bill: There was a school in Moneymohill that time that I went to and my school days were fairly all right. I remember we had a strict teacher, Miss Lane, who is not too long deceased and who was a good teacher in the school.

Mick: I went to school in Ballinahinch, New Port, County Tipperary. Those were the early days and you could say they were reasonable enough. It is different now of course because we were going to school in our bare feet in the summer time and trotting up and down the road.

Bill: That went for me too. I went in my bare feet in the month of January in the frosty weather and all. Hopping off of the road. And the roads were not as good that time as they are now. No, there would be stones and gravel and it was tricky to navigate.

Interviewer: Did you keep in touch with the friends you had at school?

Mick: Well, up to lately I did, but they are all dead now.

Bill: Yes, there would be one or two that would be living quite close to me still.

Interviewer: What was your first job after leaving school?

Mick: My first job after leaving school was I when went working with a farmer. I continued on like that for a number of years and was working for £18 for the twelve months. That was good wages that time, wasn't it?

Bill: Yes it was, better than a neighbour of mine who only got £13 the year, though he was only thirteen years too.

Mick: When I was eighteen, nineteen and twenty, the best I could get was twenty pounds a year, and that was the best that was going. Oh yeah, and you had to be a good man to get it too.

Interviewer: Bill, did you go out with a farmer after leaving school?

Bill: I had a farm of my own to try and do something with but we used also cut turf with the sleán and there was none of that machinery work like now. If you got fifty pounds for four lorry loads of good turf, you would be doing all right. I wouldn't ever consider it hard work. A brother of mine once worked the round of the day branching turf and he only eight years of age. Oh it was great healthy work. And there was nothing like the tea in the bog, you would be thirsty enough for it anyway. Tea at twelve o'clock and tea at four always. The fire would be down and the kettle would be boiled and somebody would wheel it out with a wheelbarrow.

Interviewer: What was the cutting and saving of the hay like that time?

Mick: My grandfather used to cut hay with the scythe with a couple of more men when there were no machines there to do it. They would go in there to a big field of hay and they would keep cutting away until they had it all done and if they didn't have cut it today, they would be cutting again tomorrow. They would start at about four o'clock in the morning and would work away until about twelve noon, when the real heat of the day would come. They might take a lie down until four o'clock and would then work away again until dark. That was about an acre of hay that they would cut each a day.

Bill: Later, you would cut it with the horses but you still did a lot of the turning and the saving with the pikes. There was generally seven or eight of us with pikes in the meadow at the one time shaking and turning it.

Mick: That's right. Turn the hay first and then make it into small little heaps or cocks. The next day then, if the weather had been fine of course, you'd shake it out and dry it a bit better before you'd make it into a big round winde. They were left there for a fortnight or three weeks after which they were taken in with the horse and car, or a float, and taken to the haggard and a reek made of it. There would be four, five or maybe six there the day you be making the reek; three with be horses drawing the hay in, one man forking it up and another inside forking around. Depending on the weather of course, it could take a few weeks to do. There would no hay cut that time until July anyway as there was no manure going out and it was saved during July and August.

Interviewer: What was the threshing machine like?

Mick: There was a threshing machine that was with horses that time. It was something like a big square pot and was about the height of the table. There was a spindle going out of that into a drum and there were two shafts on to this drum. There were four horses there, two to each drum and they were going around about in a ring all day with a man driving them. There was somebody else cutting the sheaves and another man feeding the machine with them all the time. After that there was a winnowing machine and it was mostly a job done at night time, and it would give you the seed, or the oats. You must remember as well that all that was cut with scythe first and when the horse mowing machine came then, it was somebody's job to go out with the scythe to cut the four corners of the meadow and the square around inside the gate where he would pull in. The two horses and machine could come in then and the man had to put a knife into it before he'd start away. They were very early days of course, but then as the years went on, you just drove in to the meadow, lay down the bar and cut away.

Interviewer: Tell me about milking the cows that time.

Mick: It was all done by hand sure the whole lot was by hand and there was no such thing as anything else. They were turned into a small little paddock or a field and they would stand outside waiting to be milked. They would be turned into the house then and you would have a stool and sit down and milk each cow. If they were hard to milk, they would put a spancel, a bit of a cord or rope, on her two hind legs. In that way she wouldn't kick and you could milk her safely. When that was done, the breakfast was eaten and it was out to tackle a pair of horses for the day and go out into the garden ploughing. At the dinnertime then, feed your horses and come back out again and plough away until six o'clock every day.

Interviewer: Bill, did you find, being a farm owner, that the times were hard?

Bill: Oh yeah, of course. There was a big grocery bill with the crowd that was there at home and there wasn't much money left over for clothes or anything after. We started making money outside the farm with the bog work like and that helped a lot.

Interviewer: Mick, when you left farming what did you move into?

Mick: When I left farming I went into working with the Board of Works. Over the last eight, nine or ten years, I got arthritis and I was not able for the travelling or heavy working on the farm so I went working with the Board of Works, working on bridges and the rivers and that sort of thing. It wasn't much and very little difference but you had to do something. I thought I might do better by leaving the farm and going to work. There was very little difference in it, there was heavy work always in feeding a cement mixer with gravel and pulling and dragging bags of cement and all that sort of thing.

Interviewer: Did the War years in the 1930s and '40s affect you?

Mick: They affected everyone that time and it was very hard to get a lot of things. It was mostly all black-market trade, for instance, if you wanted footwear or tires for your bicycle. Something that cost five shillings by the proper worth of it, if you were lucky enough to get it through the black-market, would be thirty shillings or two pounds.

Interviewer: Where was the black market in your area?

Mick: The black-market in my area was in a place called Birdhill, halfway between Limerick and Nenagh. It was just an ordinary village but it wasn't everybody that was at it. They would be brought up if they were caught selling black-market stuff, as it was seen as underhand business. If you were lucky enough to be able to get it, you would pay a pound for a quarter pound of tea.

Bill: My mother, God rest her, was a generous type of woman and she would often be giving it away to neighbours!

Interviewer: Do you remember the ration books?

Bill: Oh yeah, I do. With the crowd of us that was there, it helped a lot that the kids weren't drinking any tea, especially when it was a half-ounce of it you were getting.

Mick: People that had only two and three in a house were very hard hit but people that had families weren't doing too bad because the children would be getting their half-ounce of tea as well. It would spread a lot further. Still, it wasn't all that much.

Interviewer: What was Christmas like when you were young?

Mick: There was a bit of excitement at Christmas always. There is a lot more now than there was back then. I remember the days when you wouldn't see a loaf of bread from one end of the week to the other. All bread was baked at home and it was all cake bread. There may be a drink or two at Christmas as well.

Interviewer: Were there Wrenboys?

Mick: Oh yes, there was big bunches of Wrenboys every year. They would be collecting on St. Stephen's Day and then, maybe a fortnight after that, they might get the loan of a barn from somebody and they would have a Wren dance, as they called it. They would put on a good night indeed - bread and sandwiches and all that - and it would last all night long. It was great fun every year.

Interviewer: Was the atmosphere at home spirited coming up to Christmas day?

Mick: There was a lot more effort altogether. There is little heed put on it now because they have Christmas every day as far as I see now. Seventy years ago, Christmas was being talked of for a month before it came. The children might get some small little thing that wouldn't be costing much. There would be turkey sales at the market and they would be brought home, killed, plucked and cleaned out. Most people would have a goose instead of a turkey though.

Interviewer: What way did you find the fairs and marts in those days?

Bill: Well, fairs were different kettle of fish of course. There would be backslapping, spit-on-it and so on, and things would be generally patched up inside in the pub for a finish up. The high spirits helped on many occasions.

Mick: It was on the streets that time that the sales were and the cattle were brought onto the streets at four or five o'clock in the morning and you would be minding your own few all the time. There would be what they called "jobbers" that time to do it for you too. Cattle buyers would come along and buy out of a bunch that would suit them. The buying could go on all day from six o'clock in the morning until twelve o'clock at night. Cattle that weren't sold would be on the way home shortly after that again.

Bill: There would be about five or six fairs in the year but they would be one nearly every month in some places. The fairs in my area would be in Newcastle West, Rathkeale or Listowel. Listowel was very big but it was a bit farther away. But it was when the marts got going that they finished the fairs.

Interviewer: What else was there apart from cattle at these fairs?

Mick: There was sheep and pigs sold there too and there would be two or three market days with turkeys coming up to Christmas. Smaller animals that couldn't walk, pigs and bonamhs and all those little things, were all sold on the side of the street out of a horse and car.

Interviewer: Was there a difference between the fairs and the marts?

Mick: There was a great big difference because when the marts started, your cattle were now being weighed and they were paying so much a kilo for them. You knew what your cattle were worth where selling them on the street but you never knew their value.

Interviewer: What did you do for entertainment?

Mick: There would be dance halls in a lot of places and in the summer time, a great, big timber platform would be taken to a cross-roads and there would be dancing there until ten or eleven o'clock at night. In the winter-time, when the weather and long nights came, it was taken away and put into a hay barn or something. It would remain there until the following month of May or June when it was brought out again for the dances on Sunday nights.

Bill: In my young days, there was a travelling crowd, Gazettes from around Rathkeale, that used to show pictures. They came to the cross-roads about a mile away from us and we used to go an odd evening to the pictures there and they were fairly entertaining. There was also the dance hall in Athea and then there was the new hall that was built in Shanagolden and that was a great place.

Mick: But the sort of entertainment they had in very early days was mostly in houses, one house tonight, another house the next Sunday night and so on. There might be eight or ten or twelve that would come into a house and somebody would have a fiddle and they would dance sets in any farmers house, or in any house, on Sunday nights.

Bill: My grandmother, she played the concertina and there was such demand for her from the set dancers and so on that she used to try to avoid them! She had so much else to do, you see.

Interviewer: What influence did the coming of the television, and radio before that, have on this?

Mick: Ah sure, the television broke up the whole thing. And before that, the radio was very, very scarce. I could go back seventy-five or eighty years ago when there was a All Ireland Final on and there was only one radio for I don't know how many miles around. There was a blacksmith who had a radio and he lived with his two sisters and they had also had a radio. People would come to the house to listen to the match and there would be as much in the yard as there would be in the house. There could often be as many as thirty or forty in the yard and they listening too.

Bill: I remember that happening in our area too, houses full up with people all listening. The cows were put off until the match was played. By God, nearly everything was delayed until the match was finished!

Interviewer: Do you remember the gramophones?

Mick: Oh yes, I had one of them one time. They were great yes and there was one in my house there was for a long, long time after.

Bill: People that did have them surprised me and then it would surprise you the people that didn't have them because they were dear. We got the lend of one from my aunt, who lived to a ripe old age.

Interviewer: Was there sports or games played by you?

Mick: There would be hurling played on the fine long evenings that time, and sometimes they would play it at night! There wouldn't be a big crowd at matches in the early days of GAA except an odd time if two different club teams met and there might be a big crowd at it. But the usual turn out could be fifty, sixty or seventy or something like that.

Interviewer: How did politics feature in your life?

Mick: Ah sure, politicians are always very plentiful in every area around election time!

Bill: Of course, the leader of Fine Gael now, Michael Noonan, would be from Ballyhahill - Loughill parish. It's a curious thing that after he'd been elected for the first time he said that he would be Taoiseach. Yet, some of the staunchest Fine Gael people said that he hadn't a chance. It looks now that he has a chance all right and it isn't such an outside one either!

Interviewer: What do you recall of Troubles in Ireland?

Mick: There was six years of it that started on Easter 1916. You were dealing with an empire of course. To start off with it was an unequal conference. The ambushes started then after 1916 between the English and the Irish. There was a regiment of soldiers sent over from England and they thought they had no great trouble in defeating the few they thought was in Ireland. The bulk of the first regiment they sent went back in coffins. They sent another regiment then called the Black 'n Tans, who were a way tougher crowd altogether.They were criminals out of gaols and asylums and they were given rifles to come and shoot on sight. They used to travel around in lorries and what used happen was, some fellows at night time would go and dig a big trench across the road and they would cover it and a lorry load of them would come on next day and drive into it and half of them would be killed. That was the way the country had of fighting that time. They had guns of course and a bit of ammunition and they would travel the whole country on foot. Day and night they were ambushing.

Interviewer: Did the Black and Tans ever come into your area?

Bill: Well, I was born in September '31 so it was well over by then but I did hear that they burned Shanagolden creamery.

Mick: I was born in 1907 and I was nine years in 1916 when the fighting started on Easter. They were always in our area. They were in every area and there was the odd spy where they were able to get them. They burned plenty of thatched houses of farmers or anyone they knew that was joined in the IRA. I saw plenty of what went on.

When it started it was Ireland against England and even the women were doing as much good as what the men were. The Irish soldiers were out all night burning trains and ambushing lorries of soldiers who travelled by night. They travelled the roads without lights and you could have no lights on in your house either, except that you were able to blind it off. There was no such thing as any bit of light to be seen from the outside. They would fire from a mile across the country if they saw a bit of light and they didn't worry about who they shot.

The Tans would be ambushed at every corner and maybe the IRA might be a week waiting for them sometimes on a road. Of course they would be getting feeding from the all the neighbours around as everyone was helping them at that time.

It was a completely different story when the split came then between the Irish, when Collins and Griffith went over to England and came back with the news that they only got the Twenty-six Counties. All hell broke loose then because all the boys that were out for years before fighting for the whole of Ireland didn't get what they wanted. It split the country; brothers were practically fighting against each other. The English were giving the Free State army, the fellows that settled the difference in England with Lloyd George, ammunition. The boys in the IRA had little ammunition as it was nearly all gone and they were coming out the worst in the end of it. They had houses they could go to where there were beds ready for them and they were very plentiful. Anyone that could put them up, put them up in those days.

The two sides hated each other. One Sunday, I saw eight Free Staters dead on the side of the road and I saw another person dead inside the ditch. The IRA attacked them on the road and they shot them. But one IRA man got up with the intention to get a few guns out of the Free State army crowd that they had just shot. But there was one fellow lying on the road that wasn't dead at all and he put up his gun and shot your man the minute he put his head over the wall.

De Valera went to America at that time when the fight was on. But he let it go on and it went on for a year before he called a truce. I suppose he had right go over to England himself the first day and make the settlement instead of sending anyone else, but that was the way it went anyway.

Interviewer: I would like to thank you both for taking the time to talk with us. You have great memories.

Mick: Not so bad, I suppose, for going on ninety-four.

Bill: Michael has a fantastic memory…

Mick: …for small things that happen. In later years and I would forget them. There was a lot of hardship in those days and you wouldn't forget that.

> *September 1931: Irish Republican Army declared an illegal organisation.*
> *May 1907: John Wayne, actor, is born Marion Morrison in Winterset, Iowa, USA*

Billy Quirke - Stonemason

Because of the of the old masons continuity in stone-cutting and building throughout the nineteenth century, Limerick stonecutters and masons were first-class tradesmen and passed on their skills to their apprentices. It is generally known that Patrick Pearse's father, and brother Willie, both stonecutters, worked in St. Mary's Cathedral in the early years of the present century.

The stonecutters and masons, though closely related in terms of work and skills were, and still are, separate trades. The stonecutters generally carried out the cutting and shaping of the ornamental and finer stonework while the mason, as well as laying all the stones, cut or dressed the stonework that formed the main structure of the building. Both trades used hammer and chisels with the stonecutter using a mallet for the more delicate work and the mason a trowel in the laying process.

The masons had a secret language to their own called *"bearlagar na saor"*. Jim Kemmy, former Labour Party TD for Limerick, recalled that when he started as an apprentice to a mason in the 1950's phrases of the language were still spoken by some.

The following is an extract from an interview done with Billy Quirke of Caherhayes, Abbeyfeale, Co. Limerick, who has been a stonemason for the past half century. Billy comes from a long line of good builders...

> *"I was about eighteen when I started block work but I was twenty when I started as a stonemason proper. I worked all over Limerick, Tipperary and Kerry and the money was very tidy that time. I worked for Hanley and Robert Parkes. We used to travel*

together and petrol was cheap that time. First we stayed in digs. There was no work in or around county Limerick in the fifties and sixties and there was no buildings going up around here at all.

I did quite a lot of work in Limerick for Germans, myself, Bernie O' Connor and Phil Woulfe. They wanted stone walls built out along the Ennis road from Limerick where they had bought the houses from Hanley, the building contractor. They could get no stonemason at that time and that was in the fifties and sixties. One of the reasons for so few stone masons at that time was, I think, the lack of interest. It is hard to learn it if it's not in you. My father Michael, who I learned the trade from, built bridges and did a lot of other stonework and I did a lot of work on the Killarney road as you come into Abbeyfeale. All my brothers and uncles were involved in the building trade also.

To begin with, the stone has to be dressed and squared. Limestone is harder and it comes in a very rough state out of the quarries. Quarry stone or flagstone is easier to work with. Much of the stone I work with comes from Liscannor and Leitrim. The Leitrim stone is brown and the Liscannor is grey. I would also use stone that comes from Ballydesmond.

There were many local quarries in operation long ago. There was one in Meenkilly at Collins' (Hughes') beside the school. There was another quarry at Craig, Mountcollins and Lawrence Harnett owned it.

The phone is always ringing these days and I have to turn work down as I can't cope with it all. There is more take for stone now as opposed to the concrete blocks as stone makes a wider and nicer wall. I wouldn't like to retire I like to be working. My son

> *Liam works in the quarry there loading stone into lorries for people and my son Colm likes the buildings, but neither have a turn for stone work".*

Many of the apprentice masons in 1994 were getting a thorough grounding in all aspects of stonework at the Limerick Civic Trust project at the Ramparts section of the old city walls at Irishtown. Many new projects were under construction in Limerick and throughout the country.

Stonemasons who were once very popular in Ireland are now making a big come back. Eddie O' Riordan from Kerry trained as a stonemason recently. His grandfather had been a stonemason before him. He now has plenty of work.

Paul O'Sullivan's experience is similar to Eddie's. Ten years ago he found he could make a living from stonework alone. "*I did a lot of work in Tralee and Killarney one time but I find I hardly have to leave Caherdaniel now"* he says. He is so busy that he is forced to take on additional help when the pressure is on.

Planning regulations in south Kerry insist that most houses are faced with stone. As well as that, local authorities are demanding that garden walls surrounding houses are built of natural materials. The first course in the country to train stonemasons is being run by FÁS at the Jerome O'Connor School in Annascaul. The focus is on decorative carving although the basics of stone laying are included. There is a strong emphasis on archway building. "It is a foundation stone working course, which includes architectural stone work, stone carving, lettering and conservation" says Tim Little who heads the course in Annascaul.

Stone-masons and the building of stone walls, boundary walls around private houses and a lot of stone work in towns and villages is coming back into fashion in a big way.

Brian Curley

Since I was born on the 17th August 1927, many things have changed in Ardagh. The main street here where I live is all different now. Quite a lot of the old folk, of course, are gone, as time goes by. The people that I knew in my younger days are mostly all dead and gone. Ambroses' here next door to me used to be a pub and across the road were the Enrights, and up the road were a family of Ahernes. There are twelve of them all dead and gone, except for a grandson and a granddaughter. Barrett's shop used to do flour and meal and the like, but they're closed now. The old post offices have nobody at all living in them now. All up along the street is completely different to the way that I used to know it.

I see terrible changes in that the old people are all gone, but then again you have a new school that was built in the early '60's, and the church was built after that, and seven or eight houses have been built for the old people, which are ready to be let at any time apparently, so at least there has been progress as well. The creamery closed, of course, and that was a big loss, but then they moved to a different place. There was a joinery factory up at the top here, and the creamery took that over, and there is a big store in there now, run by Dairygold.

I started school when I was only four, and that time there was a boys' side and a girls' side and I had to start in the girls' side. I wasn't allowed in the boys' side until I was six. That school was built in 1895 and that is where I went until I was twelve. I left there then and went to the secondary in Newcastle West for two years, and that was the end of my education. I remember some of the teachers still. There was a Mr. O' Connell, and those older than me had a terrible time with him, but I was only in his room for twelve months or so, as he retired in 1936. The two teachers that came after that were Master Musgrave and Master Ryan, and they're both dead now, but they were fine. Grand harmless men they were, all they'd do was chat with themselves all day and forget about the scholar! But we all got on fine and it's all equal now at this hour of our lives. I was looking at a photograph there of us all and we going to school, and there were about ten of them dead out of it, and another five or six since. We never did much devilment and caused no harm to anybody. That is the life of it.

After leaving school, I worked at home with my father in the pub and the shop and I stayed at that until I was twenty. Then I left home to join the Wolverhampton Police. I signed up and went to Wolverhampton but I tell you, I didn't like the cut of the place! It was pure dark and dreary. Anyway, I didn't like this place known as the 'black country' at all, so I left it as it was and went off and got into the milk factory. I stayed at that for three years and then went off to work on the buildings. In 1956 I came home from England and took over the shop and the bar here. I got the post office then in 1967 and I was running the whole lot until I was sixty-five, and then I handed the whole lot over to my family. So that was my life in Ardagh and abroad. Of course, I've met all kinds, good and bad. Those were great days.

The bar trade was a lot different when I was younger, because people didn't have the money. I remember the price of the pint at nine old pence, and then it went up to ten pence or you would get three pints for a half crown. Jesus, you'd drink buckets of it at that price. You got twenty-four pints for a pound! At the change over in the coinage in 1971, which is only thirty years ago, it went up to fifteen pence a pint and look what it's climbed up to since. Times have changed no doubt, but I think that these are better days in general, because there is more money around, but you still get people robbing one thing or the other. Mind you, I remember hearing a story one day and it'll show you that there's nothing new about that! There was one man that used to call in to me there, a very funny man he was, by the name of Matt Lane. He used to work for a lady down in Kilbraderan called Maggie Hanlon, and one day he set off to Newcastlewest in her ass and cart. He got his few messages and when he was coming up Church Street, he spotted this old woman who lived out his way. So he sat her up in the back of the car and brought her on away home with him. Now, the same day, Matt was after buying lovely mutton chops off of Dan Griffin, and after dropping off the old lady and untackling the ass, didn't he discover that his fine chops were gone! So off up to the old lady's house and says he, "You bloody old mermaid, give me back my blasted chops!" She denied all round her, but do you know, she did take those chops, and her a right lady! But 'tis all equal now, as she's gone, and the man that bought the chops is gone too.

There were plenty characters like that around. We used to have beggar men that would pass through maybe three or four times a year, and they'd have a few drinks with us, sleep the night in an old shed and be on their way again. They had the same old route all the time and would just walk away with their big stick and an old bag on their backs with all their possessions. There was one that used to call here about sixty years ago, 'Hourigan the Runner' he was called, and he always said that if Limerick were properly begged, it would be worth over one and a half thousand pounds a year. And sixty years ago that was a lot of money.

There was plenty entertainment there too, of course. There used to be a dance hall here but it's a joinery works now. There used also be dances in the Old Mill and we used to walk the three miles back to it on a Sunday evening. There were also the big dances in Newcastle West, and the Deel Hall in Rathkeale, and we even went to Croom the odd time. The dance halls are all gone now, of course, and we can only reminisce about those days. We used to go to matches and the like as well, and if you went to a match in Kerry or somewhere like that, you mightn't come home at all, as you might find a dance somewhere along the way home! The first radio that came into our house was in 1938 and it was some rarity. It was electric of course, and weren't we only just after getting the electricity when they cut it off again on account of the war. Mind you, you could get the battery radio all right. The matches used to be on the radio that time, of a Sunday, so because there was no opening of the pub on a Sunday, there might be seven or eight fellows in the kitchen and you serving them away. Mind you, that time, there was a sergeant and four guards stationed in Ardagh, but then the barracks burnt down in 1958 and there was only the one left, and he not even living here. And he's gone now too. The guards are a bit of a loss, as they were mighty handy to have around. I don't remember the crossroad dances myself now, but there used to be a platform at the Daar bridge between here and Newcastle West, where Pallas Foods is now, and they used to have dances there.

In Ardagh long ago, there was this poor old man that used to live across the road from us, Jack Enright was his name, or Jack Tom as we used to call him, and he had an old gramophone. He had a stack of records and when we were children, we used to go over there of a Sunday and sit outside his sitting-room window and listen to those records for hours. He had some variety of wonderful singers. What he used to be listening to was great, but he was also a wonderful poet. God knows where they are now and it's a great pity. There was a woman living across the road from him, called Bridie Ambrose, one of the Keane Ambroses, and Jack used always sing this little song to her in his big deep voice:

"The old turf fire,
And the hearth swept clean,
There is no one half as happy,
As myself and Bridie Keane."

He had poems about the committee meetings at the creamery, and Jimmy Drew, God be good to him, used to recite them regularly. He had more about the O'Briens and Cahermoyle and the church in Kilcolman, but sure I can't remember them at all now.

I met my wife in England in 1948 and we were wed the 3rd of June 1950 and we are fifty-one years married. She's English herself but of Irish descent. We both came back over when my father asked me to, and now, as they say, Breda is more Irish than the Irish themselves. The only brother I had was killed in an accident in England in 1970, but my four sisters are all alive. One of them never married and two of the others are widows. Breda and myself had ten children, but most of them are scattered now. John has the post office alright, and his sister Mary, who works in Limerick, helps him run the bar. I gave the shop part to another son, but he's married in Limerick, and working there, so he's leased it out for now, though he still owns it.

I remember the ration books well, indeed I do. Every whole thing was rationed during the war; paraffin oil, sugar, tea, butter, meat, the lot .I can't remember what else now, but I do recall a bit of a song that was going around that time;

"God bless De Valera and Sean McEntee,
Who gave us brown bread and a half ounce of tea."

Things were so bad that if you managed to get a box of matches, you'd get a razor blade and split all the matches down the middle, so they'd last twice as long! We were lucky in one thing and that was that my mother used to get a big quota of cigarettes. Before the war and the rationing, fags were cheaper here than up in the North and my mother used to sell a load of them to this crowd that used come down for them. Because she sold so many cigarettes before the war, she was given a bigger quota of them than usual. She used to ration them out, of course, but everybody would be able to get a packet of ten.

The funerals were a big thing in those days. The cemetery is just over the wall there and people would always come into the bar after a funeral and they wouldn't go home for the whole day. But they were the days of the wakes at the house. There would always be a barrel of porter there and you'd pay your respects and sit down for a good drink. Sure, there are no wakes now. Weddings were kind of scarce, you might see two or three a year. That time, you couldn't get married during Lent, so you might see a couple of weddings on the Shrove Tuesday, just before it started. And nothing again 'till June.

We used to have a big annual fair here always, on November 21. It was always up above at the top cross there, up the hill as you go towards Carrigkerry, and that way down the Newcastle West and Shanagolden road. Where we are here on the main street of Ardagh is actually Ministerland and not Ardagh at all! There were some shocking big fairs in Newcastlewest as well. The 10th of December was the noted one, the last fair before the Christmas, so you could get a bit of money in. That's all gone now and it's a great pity. We used to love the fair day and why wouldn't we and we getting the day off school for it!

1927: De Valera signs the book containing the Oath of Allegiance and enters the Dáil with Fianna Fáil.

1950: Korean War begins when North Korean Communist forces invade South Korea.

Bridget Bond and Seán Kelly

Bridget was born in Craggard in Shanagolden in 1943 and is fifty-seven years of age. There is seven in her family and all are older than she is, and today they all live in England.

She lived out in the country and worked hard on a farm, so much so, that at the age of fourteen she left school and went into farming full time. She used to cycle up to Kilcolman to a farm where she milked cows and fed calves. They had no pigs where she worked which is just as well as she worked long enough hours from half-past seven in the morning until about six in the evening. And then she had to cycle home on her bicycle after all that.

There was one shop and a Post Office near where she lived. She used go to the shop for an old lady, Mrs Lyons, and used to get the paper and cigarettes for her. Bridget herself used to smoke a lot at one time but she gave them up.

Bridget went to school in Shanagolden where she got her Holy Communion and Confirmation and says that it was not as big an event like it is now. They had their dinner at home and that was that as they weren't very well off at that time.

She remembers her teachers, Mrs Lane, Mrs Reidy and Mrs O'Donnell, who she remembers as a very nice teacher. They used to walk to school barefoot and Mrs O'Donnell would buy ankle socks for them. They were very poor that time. They had to walk to school as there were no buses or anything that time. She liked sports when she was going to school and loved kicking ball around.

Bridget recounted a verse of a poem from school

Up the airy mountain, down the rushy glen,
We dare not go a-hunting for fear of little men,
Wee folk, good folk, trouping all together,
With green jacket, red cap and white owl feathers.

In her youth, Bridget would go to Shanagolden to play with her friends and remembers Eddie Harnett in particular. They used to have great fun at his place with cubby houses where they used to have tea and all. She used to go dancing in Foynes and Shanagolden and all the big bands were there like Big Tom and the Mainliners. Bridget went to all of them.

There was nine in the family of Seán Kelly, though three of them are dead now. He went to the old school in Shanagolden and found the teachers very good. He went working with farmers at sixteen, he worked seven years with one farmer, gave two to another and five to another. He told us that you would be working all night, half five in the morning until eight or nine o'clock at night. He said they even used to lock away the milk from them. When they'd come home after the dance they would want a cut of bread and milk but the farmers used to lock the room. They used go out and drink the milk from the tanks but then they locked the tanks on them! He used to cut and save hay with the pike, as there was no machinery that time.

Seán remembers working with the threshing machine and thought it a lot of hard work. Usually, there would be fifteen or twenty people on the machine and they would do four or five farmers in a week. Sometimes though, when they were really flying, they might do three or four in a day and on occasion they might do Ardagh in one day!

He worked in Foynes since 1972 and has seen a lot of changes there since. Working on the docks, he would bring coal and the bananas in from the boats up to not long ago. Once he fell in to the tide in Foynes one night after work but luckily a sailor found him before it was too late. Another time he fell off a house in Shanagolden and was over in Croom hospital for seven weeks. More recently, he fell in Foynes and was knocked unconscious. He was nearly killed and got eight stitches in the crown of his head and was out of work for twelve months. People compare his life to that of a cat with nine lives, he laughs.

Bridget remembers bringing coal from Foynes up the Kerry Hill on her bicycle. She said she was a fit little lady at that time, though Seán doesn't believe her.

Seán went dancing all over Limerick. He used to go to Dromkeen with Francis Kearns and he used to walk to ceilis in Kilmeedy with Frankie Bond and back down home at three or four o'clock in morning. They also walked to dances in Glin, Ballyhahill and Askeaton.

In the past, Seán said, that the Black and Tan times were tough, and Bridget remembers the ration books when they used to get small amounts of sugar and flour. Also, the great wrenparties at Dillane's in Shanagolden were something special and those great times are better than now, they said.

Both Bridget and Seán knew of holy wells in the area, especially the well in Barrigone whose pattern day is the 15th of August, and St. Patrick's well on Knockpatrick, where they go every year on St. Patrick's Day. They had heard that there were cures in the wells, but didn't think anybody had been cured by them.

Bridget recalls Christmas and getting a half crown, two apples and oranges from Santa Claus when she was young. Her family was very poor and she knew how Santa Claus worked. Easter was the same for the family and they still had nothing, though they did play the board game Ludo.

They remember the characters in the area but they are all dead now. Some told stories and Bridget said they used to say to her go to bed early because Santa Claus was coming down the chimney. A man called Jack Bond used to say to her go to bed before the fairies would come in to her.

Seán used to walk up to Newcastle to the fairs but Bridget went up with her father in the pony and trap to Crowley's that time.

Bridget has a great interest in bingo and goes to Shanagolden or Ballingarry. She used to go to Ardagh, Newcastle West, Rathkeale, Athea, Askeaton, Listowel and Ballybunion, but she gave up going to Ballybunion as it was too far back. She said she's lucky sometimes and more times she's not.

When Bridget and Seán return to Shanagolden, they can see many changes there from their youth. In Newcastle West, all the new houses and buildings have made it very different to when they called here in their early lives. Both are in Newcastle West a long time now; Seán is there twenty years and Bridget seventeen, but neither would change a thing.

---

*Joe Sheridan makes an Irish Coffee for the first time in Foynes, Co. Limerick, in **1943**.*

*The reality of the troubles in the North were brought home to those in the South when in **July 1972**, two hundred refugees from Belfast arrive in Limerick on a special train.*

Christy Brosnan

My name is Christopher Brosnan of Church Street, Dromcolliher, County Limerick. I didn't always live here but came here in 1950 and was working at Tom Twomey's in the town as a baker. In 1962, I considered I would make a move and I bought the house I'm living in now.

Speaking of Dromcolliher, there was a man there at the time of the burning of the cinema, "Paddy" we'll call him, who had rented out a house up here at that time. When the burning happened, he was put in jail for two weeks as he was responsible for it. That was 1926. There was fifty-three people that lost their lives at that burning, some of them got out but went back in again for their relatives and it was an awful disaster. It was the talk of the country for ages.

My childhood memories are of my home in Meelin, County Cork. My parents were fairly well off and my father used to keep nine or ten cows. He also had a hackney car and a nice shop in Meelin. We were classed as the middle class but there was a terrible class distinction that time between the big farmer and the small farmer and in our place it was very obvious at times.

There was no such thing as holidays for people in rural places. In Meelin, when we were young, my father and mother never went on a holiday, but when we got married here I made sure we never missed a year without a fortnight in Ballybunion, whether we could afford it or not. My wife likes travelling and goes out foreign nearly every year, Fatima last year and this year she was in Bethlehem.

I started school at five years of age and I went until I was nine and a half. I hated school and after I left I spent the rest of my time until I was fourteen years of age cutting turf in the bog. I suppose it was foolish but that was the way it went. The teachers were lovely. One man, Master Brown, lived across the road from us in Meelin. He is ninety-six years old now and we were great friends all our life. He was a great teacher, but of course he was always in and out of our house to get me to go to school. The Guards, the priests and the teachers practically lived in our house. You could do what you wanted as far as school was concerned.

As for my employers after that, well the first one I had was John Leary, who was a man in Meelin. When I started with him he was a nice man actually, but a year at the time you had to give them, and you worked hard that time. As a matter of fact I was working so hard one day that a local man came down and said "Go easy" he said " you'll kill yourself!" Ah, but I didn't mind.

My first job when I came to Dromcolliher as I said was at Twomey's Bakery. It is located across the road from where the cinema burned down in 1926. Tom Twomey was my employer there and I spent twenty-five years with him, never crossing swords once with him. He was a lovely man to work for, and anything you asked for, it made no difference in the world what it was, he got it for you. The pay was small at first, starting at fifty pence a week, after about three years I got three pounds, and after seven years it went up to five pounds. When I left in 1972 it was getting up to about nine pounds a week and I thought it great money, but it wouldn't be any good to you now.

We always had the religious days; feast days like St. Patrick's day, or any other holidays off and Sundays too but if we had to work the Sunday, we'd get holiday pay for it. There was a grand crowd working there, a master baker and four others and two thousand loaves a day we turned out every whole day. I'd be in at three in the morning and I would finish at four in the evening every day.

We cut turf for Newmarket Creamery but I remember 1947 was a hopeless year for it. That year nearly fifty loads of turf were cut but we couldn't draw it out and had to bring it out on what they call a tray. The price of a lorry load of turf then was six pounds and fifty pence and the man we used have in the bog with us would cut two lorry loads a day from seven in the morning until five that evening at twenty five shillings a day. And it was fierce hard work.

There used be pictures below in the hall from the man in Askeaton, Thossie Lee, who moved into Newcastle West after that. You might have a play once or twice in the year but around Lent, there were a lot of them on. When there was nothing on, you had to go to the hurling field and often we'd have fifty or sixty training in the field every night. There was a dance hall here called The Anchor Barn. It was built in 1947 and it was four pence for the dance and you stay there then until one o'clock. It would be full every Sunday night. Before we came here, we had a dance hall in Meelin called The Yankee Ballroom.

Christmas used be great and we had the shop that time. A week before Christmas they would start carrying home their messages and everything on horses, donkeys and cars. I remember one day in 1939, a woman carried a Christmas order from us worth eleven shillings and six pence. We couldn't get over it! People would be coming all week up to Christmas Eve and even on the night, up to twelve o'clock there and then you wouldn't see them again for a week. My parents would up shut the shop at twelve o'clock and my mother would go to mass. She was a very holy woman but my father was the opposite and wasn't that holy at all.

I like to go mass on Sunday morning and it doesn't matter where we get it. Religion played a big part in my life but I'm the class of man that's not a fanatic about it but I still wouldn't miss mass on a Sunday. To treat people right and to be straight and honest with them and no more about it is the way I live life. I always thought that I would like to be a priest but it never materialised after.

My mother used always be talking about the Black and Tans, and a great rebel man in Meelin, Paddy McCarthy. He ran with the famous Sean Moylan's gang but was shot in Millstreet after. So the Tans were around and there were three houses to be burned in Meelin; one of them was my mother's, then Quinlan's pub and Callaghan's also. They were just eating their Christmas dinner when the Tans came and ordered them all out of the house so they could burn it to the ground. They did so and as a result, there was a big ambush in Meelin that evening, when the Tans were coming along the road. There was a big log put in their path and the local lads fired down from the hill but they missed them.

At home, we were always for Fine Gael and all belonging to me were Fine Gael. My father was a huge supporter and many meetings were held in our house in Meelin. One night there was a big meeting on and they had to bring out the army because they thought that there would be murder at it but it passed away quietly. Politics in Meelin that time was a fright and you couldn't say a word to anyone as they could be in the IRA and you wouldn't know.

Dromcolliher then was a big place for Fianna Fáil and one time De Valera, at the start of his career, said he would come to Dromcolliher. There was a man back the road, Lord Muskery, who was very involved in politics and there was a big meeting called above in the square when Dev came and Muskery was first to speak to the crowd. He started off "Reverend Fathers, ladies and gentlemen. We had reptiles among us but they are gone in the name of Saint Patrick but this evening, we have a great reptile among us here by the name of Eamon De Valera!" And with that, they took him off the platform and sent him off back home. The following night a knock came to his door and three hooded men carried him down to Cappawhite in

County Tipperary. They told him not to ever again get involved in politics. So that was the finish of Lord Muskery and politics and I think that was back in 1932.

I started athletics when I about thirteen years of age when I joined the sportsclub in Meelin. There was a man there that time, Tim Joe Connell of Knocknagree, who was an Irish champion that year. He inspired me to later win the County novice, junior and senior, Munster novice, junior and senior and an All-Ireland junior. But it was always my ambition to go back and start an athletics club in Meelin and we did start one since.

In 1960, I won the six-mile Cork County senior title but after that I didn't run a whole lot as I got hurt somewhere along the line. I did a few road races and won the one in Newcastle West for the Finsale Cup. That was my main achievement and I was made a sports star for it. I would love to go to all the athletics I could and of course all the hurling and all the football.

I am a true Cork man but my children are real Limerick supporters, oh God, they are a terror! We can't all be in one house watching a match, especially if it is Cork and Limerick. There was only one game to play in Meelin when we were young and that was hurling. We had no field to play in but then no one else had a field that time either. We would go into a neighbour's field to play but when he would come home in the evening we'd be cleared out of it. There was a field all right in Newmarket and that was three miles away.

Unfortunately we never won many matches but I can recall back in 1944, we had a lovely team in Meelin. They went down to play Millstreet in the final and the first day it was a draw, which I thought Meelin won by a point, but at the replay they murdered one another completely and we were suspended for a long time after.

My brother died six months ago of cancer and he was in America. Three of the family went to America so there are two of them there now, but they were home last year after fifty years. They couldn't get over the prosperity and everything in Ireland. When they left at that time, it was America and that was that. The night before they left, I remember, we had an American wake and all around would come to it for the sing-song 'till the morning, and then some good singer would sing "The Shores of America". They would get up early in the morning and head off to the train in Newmarket. And that was it. You were gone then and there was no more about you. The people that time thought it a fright going to America, as though it was something worse than death!

I remember the funeral wakes too, going back a good bit. My father had the hackney car that time and we would go back the country to a place called Toureenfineen and we would get the clay pipes and the snuff for the funeral. Everyone would remain all that night and the following day until eight that evening when the corpse would be carried away. And everybody there, bar a nun, would be drunk. That's a fact and that was the way it was always. If they could keep the corpse for two or three days they would. It was an awful sensation when a person would die that time, whether they were old or young, as it took awful effect on the whole parish. All tools would be downed and the whole lot would be on ponies, traps and saddle ponies and would be there for three or four days. Sometimes, people even came just for a good time! That was the way the wakes were.

If there was a wedding in the area we would all get made up with straw and would go out strawing. What it meant was that we would arrive at the house of a newly married couple and we knocked at the door and if they didn't allowed us, or had no idea what we were up to, we would have to go home. But it never actually happened. You would ask the bride out to dance in her own kitchen and we would stay for the night there for a bit of a party. That custom was in Meelin but not in Dromcolliher at all. They are all gone out now and it's a pity because they were great.

I knew my wife for ages before we married. My father died in 1956 and back then you would have to stay inside for twelve months and there was no more about it. After the twelve months was up, I came on to this lady at a dance one night. I knew her well and we danced away and I asked her that night if she would go out with me and she said she would and from that on it came.

She was working in Kanturk and I was working here in Dromcolliher and after six years I decided that I would pop the question and she said yes. We will be married thirty-eight years on 2nd July 2001. In two years time we will go to Medjugorje if we can. But God knows they were nearly forty years of greatness and it has been like forty days and let's hope we will be there for the next forty.

1950: Charles Shulz introduces the Peanuts comic strip, featuring Snoopy.

1972: Donny Osmond has a number one hit with Puppy Love, quiffs and hairspray are the order of the day for all the boys, and Mastermind and Columbo make their debuts.

Dan Gayer

My name is Dan Gayer of Feenagh, Kilmallock, County Limerick. It's a Cork name, and all my ancestors came from County Cork, around the Mallow side. It would have been my grandparents that moved down here. I was born, bred and reared in this house in Feenagh, as were my father before me and his father before him. My mother and father were here in this house until they both died. My father died at the age of eighty-four and my mother at about seventy. She was formally from Croom.

There were only two sisters and myself in the family. My two sisters are gone to their eternal reward long ago so I am an only boy and spoiled. My father kept me to learn his trade. He was a harness-maker and had a bicycle shop also. In the evenings when I'd come home from school I had to help him, learning the leather and repairing and building new bicycles. I kept that on for a long time.

I remember I was going to school and I heard a mowing machine coming up the road one day. It was Paddy Keogh from Kilmeedy with a horse-drawn mowing machine. I could hear the click of it and I went out to the big gate and he stopped outside and he put his hand in his pocket and he gave me a big brown penny, which he put on the gate, that was the time when you got 240 pence for a pound. Ever afterwards, when I would think it was Paddy Keogh coming again, I would be looking forward to another big brown penny.

Things are a bit different now, though. The corncrake was lovely to hear in the morning and at night. They are trying to bring him back again but the cutting of silage finished them all. When I travelled up to Galway they used not call the hay "windes" at all but "trams" and they would have no float either to carry them only put a big "*súgán*" (hay rope) around the bottom of the winde and pull it along. They would make a row of them then in the middle of the field and never have them spotted all over the field.

I started school around 1925 and I served under four teachers. Master Power was the old man that was there and the head teacher. Jack Mahony, formally from Dromcolliher, was the assistant. Sean O'Leary, the third teacher, came from Kenmare, and Master Scully from Dromcolliher was my last teacher. The school was at the end of the village in those days but it is the community hall now.

There were many children going to school that time. For the last two years I spent with Master Scully in Feenagh, my job in the morning was to get my slate and count every class. Up to one hundred pupils from the boys in Feenagh, not to mind the girls. We had a great time and Master Scully had a great time and I often congratulated him afterwards. When he retired, I would often meet him when I would go to Dromcolliher. "Ah Dan," says he "I struck a good time when I came from Kilmeedy to Feenagh. I had great pupils. They were all geniuses. They were all priests, doctors, inspectors and professors, no bother to them." I met several of the pupils afterwards but a lot of them are gone now. All of my class are gone now, I'd say, except myself.

When Jack Scully came to Feenagh from Kilmeedy in 1934, I remember it well. He had a motor bicycle, as he was the head teacher, and he kept me on for two years in the school even though I had nothing to do! He kept me to correct the home exercises for the lower classes. We were great friends. My father didn't want me to go to college and the assistant teacher, Jack Mahony, said to my father to, "send Dan to engineering". I wasn't too stupid and I was mechanically minded.

I finished school at the age of sixteen and my father kept me at home. I was at his trade until his business went slack. With the advent of motor cars and tractors, there wasn't much work for harness-makers. The harness making was in the slated part of the house. We built on to it, you see, and my father worked in the far down part of it. Even when I was working at the trade my father kept at it. He was working up to the very last as he was good and healthy.

A farmer came one day to make new winkers for the horse. "I'll call back for it when it is ready in a week," he said as he left. So the farmer called back "Have you the winkers made?" "I have," replied my father. "I can put it on myself when I go home", said the farmer. "Oh, you should have told me," says my father " because it was for the horse I made them!" He had a good sense of humour and I got a bit of it from him, I suppose.

In our place, we had the harness making and the bicycle sales and I had a small electric unit. We had our own electricity before the E.S.B. came in 1950. We had our own current and we charged the batteries for all the old radios. I used charge the wet battery for all the users around and it was very interesting work.

Then when the electricity came in around 1950 I started fitting milking machines here, there and everywhere in Kerry, north Cork, Clare, Tipperary and throughout County Limerick. I was mostly in sales and I sold milking machines to farmers for ten years. When the sales of the milking machines went down, when all the farmers had been supplied, I switched over to selling farm buildings, hay sheds, milking parlours and all kinds of buildings. I went back to the people that I had sold the milking machines to and they were all happy with my previous business and I scored again and sold buildings to the people I had sold milking machines to! I had a great time going around, getting grub and liquor wherever I went. If I was a drinker, I could be drunk every day of the week!

I was on the machines and then the farm buildings up to about ten years ago. Then the companies that I was working for closed down, there was a recession with the farmers for a few years, and things were not going so well.

During my travels selling the milking machines, I was travelling outside Killarney one day and I didn't know where I was going. I met an old woman on a donkey and car about a mile outside Killarney. I stopped and asked her for directions to this certain farmer. "Oh," says she "it's only a mile and a bit down the road". The bit was fifteen miles! And says she, "what would you be asking for him for?" I told her that I was selling a milking machine to this man and I couldn't stir, my car was stopped and the donkey was right across it, it was a narrow road and I couldn't stir until she got all the information! I enjoyed it so much there that when I arrived at the customer I fitted the machine and I stayed there for the week.

I travelled down to West Clare, out to Loop Head, and went up to the light-house. There I was, in the next parish to America, so I met people everywhere.

I was sent to Valentia Island off the coast of Kerry. I had to go across by boat and the first man I met when I arrived over was Mick O'Connell, the famous Kerry footballer, who was working in an American cable station at the time. I asked him where could I get a car on the island, as it was about three miles long. "Ah," says he, "you will have to walk it. There is only one car in the place, at the post office, but the post-master will drive you out to the farmer". I got there anyway and got back safe and sound.

Then I travelled down to west Cork and another time out to Whiddy Island. I had to go across in a boat and I sold three machines the same day, as they were after getting an underground cable of electricity from the main-land out to the island, and I had a great time out there too.

I travelled all over Ireland but never went across the sea. I didn't find any change when the electricity came in. I had a generator before the E.S.B. came. I wired most of the houses around the place. I could do wiring or anything like that. I was a general handy man, a chancer. I remember I wired a house for this poor old woman and she had a lovely Sacred Heart paraffin oil lamp up on the wall. I wired up an electric one and when I was finished then, " Dan", says she " how often do I have to put the paraffin oil now in the electric lamp?" Innocent out!

We had two good fellows, two experts, next door to us. BJ Sexton, he could do anything, and my own fellow, working with the steel, was every bit as good. It is all steel work he does, welding and repairing that way, but it's hard to tune him, you'd have to come round him the easy way.

When I was going to school, there was the world of industries in the place. From the creamery, which is now a garage, they were selling coal and taking the milk, and it was a meeting place for all the farmers. In the village then you had four or five shops and there was about ten thatched houses. There was one petrol pump just below the Village Inn and I can remember the petrol was sold at "one and six pence" a gallon and 'R.O.P.' was written over the fan light which meant "Russian Oil Produce".

There was another bicycle mechanic repairing near the church. You had three public houses, a draper, confectionery shops, cobblers, and stone masons. A lot of them could be revived again. There is a great opening here now for a tailor, a shoe repairer, a stone mason or a barber. The last blacksmith that was here was Jack Brosnan. He took it over from his uncle, who was trained there as well, but they are all dead and gone.

An O'Gorman man down through the years was the thatcher, then there was this present fellow now and his father before him, and his father before him, as far back as 1878 nearly. There was another thatcher, John Meaney, and he was from Glenduff, near Ashford. He was a kind of fellow working for nothing but 30 bob a day. A thatcher nowadays is £80 or more a day. John Meaney was training young FÁS trainees. I don't know whether it fell through or what. If the house was thatched properly it would be done for twenty years. I won't be here for the next time and it is sprayed now and the thatcher that is doing it, he is very good. He is spraying it with blue stone and we tried everywhere to get it, and above at James Wall's I got it. He has everything in Dromcolliher. If you wanted anything and you couldn't find it anywhere, call into James Wall and you will get it.

I would say the big house above here is the oldest one in Feenagh but as far as I know, this house here is at least two hundred years old. It is the only thatched house left here and it will be kept that way while I'm alive.

For entertainment, I used to join up with the local Macra or Pioneer movements. One day a Pioneer crowd of us went to Killarney on an outing. I was always asking questions and we went out on the jarveys out to the lakes. I asked the old jarvey driver when we were going by the racing track what that place up there was. "Ah", says he "that's the place where they gallop horses and greyhounds". "And do you ever go to the races?", I asked. "I did", he said "and I will never forget one day when I backed a horse at twenty to one and he came in at a quarter to three!"

I am a pioneer all my life and never drank nor smoked. I am nearly fifty-eight years a pioneer now. Jim Neenan of Broadford joined me up. He was the organiser for the Pioneers through the head office in Dublin, then we had a parish Priest or a curate, Fr. O'Dea, who was spiritual director down through the years. Many of my pals who joined then are all dead and gone now. I was in the pioneer committee but now they are all gone. There is only a lackadaisical committee here today and a lot of them are wearing the pin and, not judging them, they will turn the back of the coat when they go into a pub.

There was a dance hall next door to us known as Sexton's Hall. I never danced much in my youth but I would stand at the door watching. I wouldn't be left in as I was underage at the time. I was spotting, I suppose, and the rest of it.

There used to be a travelling cinema over near the creamery, at a place called the Cass, where they showed all the old cowboy films. I remember these two local fellows and they were in the pub but they were put out and they decided to go to the pictures. At the cinema, the back seats were higher up and you had to pay more there for the better view but these two old fellows, anyway, they were half jarred when they went in and they were put out in the front row seats. There was a cowboy film being shown and a big flock of cattle and horses came running onto the screen. All of a sudden, one of the fellows pipes up, "come on lads," says he, "get back or we'll be trampled here!" They thought they were coming out on top of them, innocent out!

The church here originally was a thatched house and there is a plaque inside in the hallway. It was in olden times, I don't know when, before my time, and the two wings were built on to it. It was only the straight aisle that was there originally. Ah, that is well over one hundred years ago now, I would say.

Religion played a big part in our lives. When we were preparing for our First Holy Communion we had a cranky old parish priest. He was a lovely man really, but you couldn't say everything to him at all, so we had mock confessions preparing for the proper confessions. I remember one fellow went in before me to confession and the Priest shouted at him, "speak out and tell me your sins." "I bate an ass, father!" said the boy. Well if he did, the priest cleared him out of the box!

For Confirmation then, we had a red catechism, a green one and an Irish one, but we never used the Irish one. We would be called up around the desk with Master Scully and we would all count our own question. He would start with me, he would go round one way, and I would just learn the first question. That was grand for a few days, but on this day, didn't he start at the other end and the fellow there answered my question. You see, he had spotted what we were up to and we were sent down to our desks and we had to stay in for play-hour. But when play-hour came we all stood up and walked out. He said nothing, as he was a pure gentleman.

I had an uncle, John Gayer, who lived in Patrickswell. He is dead and gone too, but he was very brainy. In his young days, he worked in the British Treasury in England. He was a great hurler and the last hurling match he played was against another Irish team outside in London with the famous Michael Collins. It was the last that Collins played before he came home to Ireland in the Trouble Times.

My uncle then, with another man from Kilfinane, his name was Brazell, went about coming home. My uncle got a return ticket and he convinced the English people that he was coming back again to England but he never did. The fellow that was with him only got a single ticket and he was stopped at the customs and sent back. He was put into the British Army and he was shot at the first line of trenches out in France afterwards. That is what saved my uncle; he had the brains and he bluffed them.

They had the ration books during the War and there was a song about it but I forget it now. I often went to Croom then, where they were selling the tea and sugar on the black market. I used get it for the neighbours at a pound for the tea and sugar.

I used to deal with farmers a lot, but I never thought of getting into farming because, I suppose, I was born for the job of interviewing people and talking to them and trying to cod them or bluff them or whatever.

I have a son and he was always with the neighbour across the way after leaving school. He is a great cattle man, a great judge of cattle, and he would love to have a farm and maybe, in time, he will. I had an uncle in Patrickswell and he had a farm, though he was not a good farmer. He was more of a gentleman farmer, you know, going according to the book. No one in the family had an interest in the trade I was in, the harness making. They are all out in jobs and I couldn't teach them when they hadn't an interest in the thing.

There have been a lot of changes for the better. Almost nobody is short of money now but the more they get, the more they want.

1925: Border Commission agrees to maintain existing borders and De Valera questions the absention policy adopted by others towards the Dáil.

1950: Ian Paisley forms the Free Presbyterian Church.

Dan Joe O'Riordan

My name is Dan Joe O'Riordan of Killarney road, Abbeyfeale and I was born on the Main Street, where 'Bobby's Bar' is now. It was on the 26th May 1921, supposed to be five days after the attack on the barracks in Abbeyfeale.

I had four brothers, but one died when we were young, and I had five sisters but one of the sisters died when she was young as well. The brother was the eldest in the family but one day, when they were cooking gruel or porridge or something up in range, he pulled the pot off the range and scalded himself, and died as a result. My sister was nearly a teenager when she died. I think her clothes caught fire from a candle as she was coming out of her bedroom. Some of her older sisters saw her but could do nothing about it.

I then had three brothers and four sisters left. My father ran the pub that is now Bobby's Bar, but then it was Riordan's, or 'The Long Bar', as it was known. He died when we were all young, in 1928. I was gone seven years of age and I remember being in the graveyard with my mother and she was crying. I did not know what was happening, with the result that I now have no memory of my father.

I went to school down at the local Community Centre, on what is now Church Street, for seven or eight months of the year. They were tough times, and we barefoot going to school, but we thought nothing of it. I went as far as seventh or eight class but I remember there were four classes in the one room when we came to the last teacher. He was Joe Hanley, the Lord have mercy on him. Fifth, sixth, seventh and eight classes all in the one room under the same old school master.

He was exceptional as a teacher. I remember, one day, we were learning something to do with English and he asked this question and we were all wrong, not one of us answered correctly. He asked it a second time and I gave an answer the others hadn't answered previously. I answered even though I was in fifth class and there were fellows there much older and bigger than me. I must have been correct as he called me up to his desk and what did he say to me? This is worth laughing at – he said, "I'd give you my daughter only she is going to be a nun". He had only one child and she was a lovely girl and I would have loved to have had her. But she didn't become a nun and she married but I don't know whether she is dead or alive today. She was a beautiful girl and I felt so proud that day and "I'd give you my daughter only she is going to be a nun" lives with me to this day.

After the national school, my mother sent us to secondary school. We cycled from the Main Street, Abbeyfeale to Saint Michael's College in Listowel and home again. We had five days a week in school and a half-day on Saturday. Out in the morning with our bottle of milk and our bits of bread and butter, that is all we had. Bad bikes, bad roads and no rain gear. And the milk would often be sour but we couldn't care less, we were used to drinking sour milk. You'd laugh and why wouldn't you, those were the times that were there.

We had nothing else, currant cake maybe at Christmas and lucky to have it, and there was another thing my mother, God rest her soul, had for us on Christmas, seed cake we used to call it. It was lovely altogether.

I got a scholarship from Limerick County Council as a result of my Leaving Cert. in Listowel to an Agricultural School. So I went to Clonakilty and I had experiences there because, in our turns, we got one week milking cows and another week we'd be feeding the calves and there was another week in the piggery and then a week with the poultry.

We'd study in the mornings till after lunch and then we'd work. We had to do everything physical; cutting beet, crowning beet in the wintertime and the hands falling off of us with the cold. I'll never forget it, I can't forget it because in the College we were enclosed and we were only allowed out on Saturday afternoons to do shopping in Clonakilty town, which was about three miles away. We had to walk there and if we walked there (twenty-eight of us by the way), we had two House Masters with us just in case we would do anything out of the way. But it still didn't prevent us from meeting a few girls in the town and arranging for a night out to the pictures. But though the House Masters would still be with us, we'd have already arranged it with our girlfriends to meet them in a certain seat so there was nothing the Masters could do about it.

At the end of the year I got another scholarship to spend three years as a forestry trainee at Avondale in Wicklow. I'll never forget it. But then, before I could get started on that, I was called to the University for Dairy Science, based on the result of my final exam in Clonakilty. They wanted to know whether I'd accept it or not. At that time, the whole forestry thing was only getting started, back in 1942. So anyway, I waited and I rang my mother, and the phone calls were dear enough, and I told her to enquire from the Dairy Produce Inspector who was living outside here somewhere near Fealesbridge, O' Connor, I think was his name, to find out his advice on what I should do. So he advised me to take the dairy science and go to the university. The difference then was, you see, at the university I'd have to pay for myself and the other one was all free. Three years and everything was free and I suppose I knew my mother wasn't that well off. There were so many more of us there and I didn't like putting the expense on her. But she still wanted me to do the dairy science and so I did. I got through it and it came close to our finals, which were in March, and that Christmas, I came home on holiday and my mother, God rest her, she had a fire in the sitting room, every day for me to study.

The morning I was going back after the holidays, I went to Eccleston's corner and I gave a look back and I saw my mother still standing at the door, and I cried, not at the thought of leaving her but at the thought of not passing my exam. I knew what it meant to my mother. Anyway, the next March I did my final and I got it. It meant everything to me and it meant everything to my mother.

After leaving the university, I worked in Adare, on sickness duty as the assistant manager was off sick and I was asked to do it at that time because there were so few people qualified. The Irish government was only just getting into doing business like the Forestry and the Dairy Science.

I stayed working in Adare under Bishop Casey's father, who was the Creamery manager in Adare and I suppose there is no harm in saying it, I got to know some his family. Bishop Casey, of course I had to get to know him and I got to know one of his sisters. I went out with her a few times and when it came for my time then to finishing up in Adare, what did my girlfriend do, Bishop Casey's sister, only asked her father to try and keep me for another week or two! Oh, I am not blowing now. She's dead since, the Lord have mercy on her. She was married in Cork and I saw her a few years ago.

Newport in Tipperary was my next stop, again doing relief work, but it was all experience. I was in Kantoher next, for quite a while, and then I was in Broadford, which was the biggest branch creamery in the country at the time. I was doing relief sickness duties there again to a Jack Quinlivan.

The working day was from eight in the morning until five or maybe half five in the evening, but we got good money for doing holiday relief duty. We could nearly ask what we wanted. They wanted us so badly, they paid our digs and all. Well then I went to Askeaton, again doing cover for somebody off sick, and what do you know, but they offered me a permanent position.

It was my first offer of a permanent job and I asked them the rates, I will never forget it. Three pounds a week plus a five shilling bonus for Sunday, and an extra five bob bonus, and I never asked what the five bob bonus was for! I was out in digs and we'd have to cycle about three miles into work and at the end of the year in Askeaton, I got twenty-five pounds at Christmas, by the way of a cheque bonus. It was some amount of money, oh yes! I was only paying fifteen shillings a week for my digs.

I used to come home every weekend, to see my mother, God rest her. I used to come home every weekend without fail, no matter where I was, for the simple reason I felt I made her happy and I felt myself happy anyway, after seeing her.

I had plenty to do. I had a General Manager who did the detailing of the work, but I wasn't happy unless I was involved in what all the other workers were doing. I bagged coal and I bagged turf, and that time we used to buy all sorts of things from the farmers. Hides, feathers, poultry, eggs, horsehair, you name it. Anything the farmer had to sell we bought it from them, even dead hens! We had a market for them all. We used to sell the wool to Scottish wool growers, through an agency in Limerick. We bought and sold everything that the farmer would bring into us, apples and other fruit, and reeks of turf. We also ploughed for the farmers, as we had the machinery and the workers to operate them. Before that, up until 1944, there was nothing only milk being bought in that creamery, but after 1945, when I first arrived, the place really expanded. We also formed an association for the creamery managers in West Limerick. We knew we were up against it, because a whole lot of the managers in the West Limerick area were unqualified, they had no qualifications what so ever. The first qualified men from the University were in 1928. I got to be Assistant Honorary Secretary in the West Limerick branch. Any problems that the managers had in Limerick or Kerry used to come to me at the Association. We were also one of the first creameries in Ireland to export cream to London.

I had good times but I worked hard for what I got. I decided to retire back in 1983.

It wasn't all work with me, though. When I was younger, I used to frequent St. Ita's hall of a night, playing cards and billiards and snooker. That time St. Ita's was known as the Catholic Young Men's Society (CYMS) hall. You paid an amount to become a member, but it wasn't much, and after they got to know me, they made me the treasurer. I'd go dancing, then, up to Tom Tobin's, and it was three old pennies to get in, from eight o'clock in the evening until eleven that night. And if you didn't have the three pennies, he'd let you owe it to him till the next day. My mother, God rest her, would have a mug of milk and two or three buns for me after the dance, then I'd jump on my bicycle and head back to Askeaton, and think nothing of it. There was a place between Rathkeale and Askeaton that was supposed to be haunted and for a while I was in dread of my life of it. I used to always say a few prayers!

I joined the L.D.F. at the outbreak of the Second World War and I suppose a share of us joined to get clothes and shoes. We got them free! I got to be an intelligence officer. They sent me down to Youghal to do a course during my summer holidays and I came home a qualified intelligence officer in the L.D.F.! Our role was to find out what to do if anyone came to attack Abbeyfeale. The first morning I was in the training camp, I'll never forget. I got up when the bell was going off, at around at 6 o'clock in the morning. I went to the bathroom and toilets and looked for hot water to shave, and the army officer asked me where did I think I was, that this was not a hotel! The result there was no such thing as hot water. Every morning I put my head under the tap and I had to wash with cold water, and ever since it's in cold water I wash. I'd put my head under the tap even if there was ice in it.

I was transferred when I went to the university, from Abbeyfeale to the 48th Battalion in Cork City until the war was over in 1945. I have a citation I was given from the Minister for Defence and a service medal. We got no payment for being in the LDF, nothing at all, except a pair of boots and a military uniform.

I don't remember any stories about the War of Independence or the Civil War, but I suppose we were so young and we weren't so interested in these things. I'd say anyway we didn't see what was going on, we were only anxious about ourselves. We'd be put off the street in the winter time when we were young, at seven o'clock, and nine o'clock in the summer time, anyway, there was no street lighting that time. I suppose we were controlled by our parents. I had one sister Eva, she ended up being Jim White's wife, and she had us kneeling at our bedside every night for our night prayers. Of course they were mad about De Valera here in Abbeyfeale, as it was a rebel town you know. I'd say our house at the time was a republican house with the result that we were all Fianna Fail, in other words, we were on de Valera's side, though through no fault of our own. It just developed when we saw the way things were happening.

I'm living here in the Killarney Road since 1964 and it has had a great bearing on my life. I'd be dead long ago only for '64 happening. 'Tis sad the way I'm going to relate it now, but my mother died in 1964 and that started it. I had tried everything to give up cigarettes during many Lents and it failed me. I never had health while I was smoking. On several Lent times, I'd give away my fags on Shrove Tuesday night and I'd be looking for a butt the next morning. But when my mother died I said I had to do it for her. I gave up smoking for my mother and if you gave me twenty thousand pounds today to smoke a fag, I wouldn't do it and it's a lot of money. I know the harm they can do. I'd be dead long ago, only for giving them up. I put it down to my mother, and the prayer with it. I have a rosary said before I get out of bed every morning, before half six.

I went all the way to Dublin for my wife! She was working with one of the sisters above in Cleary's order office and came down home for a visit with her during their holidays. I had a girlfriend at the time, but when they went back to Dublin, we started corresponding, and the next thing, I went up to Dublin to meet her. I took one of my brothers with me, just in case, and that's how it all got started!

The children have it much easier nowadays, everything is done for them. We had nothing when I think of it but then again, we had everything, because we were happy with having nothing, because there was nothing there to have.

1921: The Mayor of Limerick, Ald. George Clancy, ex-Mayor Micheal O'Callaghan, and volunteer Joseph O'Donoghue, are all shot by British Crown Forces, in front of their families. Dáil representatives and Lord Mayors from around the country attend the funeral.

1945: End of the Second World War and the Congress of Irish Trade Unions is formed.

David Ambrose

I'm David Ambrose and I was born in Churchtown, Newcastle West, onto a farm. There were ten children in the family - five boys and five girls.

My father was a farmer. They were rough times back then, and with only twenty-five acres and with the milk only a shilling a gallon that time it was very tough, but we just got along and everybody helped each other.

I went to school in Newcastle West at Courtenay Boys School, on Bishop Street. Some of the teachers were tough, not like nowadays. I got my primary certificate in 1959 and I left there and I went to the technical school up the road for two years. After that I left and got a job in the mineral water factory, Nash's Mineral Waters. I worked there for two years, washing bottles and bottling minerals, Guinness and other beers. Sometimes I got to go out on the trucks delivering.

The wages that time were very small, roughly one and six an hour, that would be about thirty-six pence an hour. I left there then in October 1963, at the age of sixteen, and I emigrated to America. I was only over there a month when John F. Kennedy was killed. I will never forget that as long as I live.

My first job in America was when I worked in green houses, growing plants on about four acres of land. This woman that we worked for, Patricia Murphy, had two restaurants down in Manhattan in New York. She also had one big restaurant in Yonkers, outside the Bronx, where I worked and we grew and designed all the flowers for this one restaurant.

I worked forty-eight hours a week at that time. We were considered farmers with that type of wage. The wage was poor but I liked the work.

The way of life there was different to here. For example, the television was just coming out in Ireland when I was leaving. There was one television down the road from me and everybody would go to that house to watch it at night-time. Over there everybody had a set.

On the fair days, when we were kids, we would take off our sandals and our socks and walk through all the stuff on the ground. All the Yanks and visitors would be around and they would be out looking at the cattle and the cows and seeing us running around. It was all happening in the square in Newcastle West right up until the sixties. They would be on once a month but the big one I think, was on December 10th, if I'm not mistaken.

My grandmother, she was a great old lady, Lord have mercy on her. She used to pluck the chickens and the turkeys for all the people in town. And my grandfather was in the British Army and he fought in the Boer War. At the time of the troubles with the Black and Tans, they were going to burn some house down one time and my grandfather came out to this British officer. He showed him his medals and the officer said that this man had nothing to do with any troubles or anything like that and the house was safe that time.

There is another man up in Churchtown there who has a farm, James Woulfe is his name, and his father was known as "Angle" Woulfe. One day he was coming home from the creamery and he smoking and he started coughing. Some old lady stuck her head out the door and she says "Angle, that's a graveyard cough!" He says back to her, "there's many people inside the grave that wish they had that cough!"

We had one teacher in national school, Joe Shea, and he was always telling us not to smoke. He'd get a fag and he'd cough into a handkerchief, a clean handkerchief, and he'd show you that the handkerchief had gone a kind of yellow. Then there was Ned White, he was my next teacher and he was a very quiet man. His wife lived right down the road from us and she was a hairdresser and a mid-wife. She'd probably have delivered my brothers and sisters. There was no such thing as going to hospitals those days.

Sometimes after you read the paper you'd wonder what you'd be eating. Long ago there was nothing like that. One year, my mother raised a big load of turkeys, about fifty or so. Anyway, the same year, the price of turkeys went down. They hardly paid her to raise them. But guess what we had for dinner every Sunday? Turkey! But the fox came and took the last three or four of them and we were delighted. You' get tired of the same thing.

I never knew my grandfather on my father's side of the family. He owned a farm up in Kileedy. There was a big old beautiful house up there in Churchtown belonging to my grandaunt. Anyway, my grandfather was visiting her one day with a horse and car and himself and another guy stopped off for a couple of drinks on the way home. They were going outside the town, up the Cork road, and they met the Black and Tans. Something was said anyway and next thing a shot was fired and it went through the trap and hit my grandfather in the leg and hit the other one in the leg too and the two of them bled to death. There is some kind of plaque up there for the two of them on the Cork road.

My grandmother remarried again and she raised two families, about fifteen or sixteen kids between the two families. I had an uncle, he's dead now, Lord have mercy on him, Tony, and they used to call him 'Sandyman Port', and he was a terrible character altogether.

Major Tully was another great character who lived in a small house which was part of where O'Neills Furniture shop is today. He was in the Boer War too and himself and my grandfather were great friends. He was a bit larger than life and he married a Portuguese woman. And the rants every day…

He would put on a big war bonnet and him with his big beard and he'd put the wife into the pram and off he would go around the town. I got that war bonnet when he died.

My uncle and my father used to go back to the bog for the turf during the war times. Things were so hard then that they used to cut timber from there and sell it around the town. There was no coal there, because it wasn't coming in on the ships as they were being bombed. I often remember the big long cross-saw. I think it's still over in the cowshed, really old it is, and back and forth it used to cut the timber. One time my father and my uncle were at the bog and they were burning some of the area, the old heathery stuff, and it got out of control. My father broke the handle of the shovel trying to put it out, but never got it all out. They were going down the road anyway when the met a man and he said to them, "Jesus, there's a lot of smoke back there! What's going on?" My father says "I know nothing about it" and kept going!

I was in the gardening business from 1963 to 1965 and then I got called for the American Army in November '65 and was stationed in New Jersey, at Fort Nix. They took us to Philadelphia to get a plane. I was looking out the window and I saw this old plane outside. I thought it was a relic, it was like something out of a museum. What I didn't realise was that we were getting on it! We got on the plane anyway, as we had to fly out to Colorado. There was a lady, a stewardess, on board, and I got talking to her and she said she was from Tipperary. But as I was talking, whatever look out I gave, the engine was on fire.

We had to make an emergency stop in Missouri. We all got off there but there was nobody in charge of us. The first thing was to find the nearest bar. And there were guys there that night that drank and they never drank before. It was such a scare, but they got us another plane and they flew us out to Colorado. There I did six weeks of basic training and they flew me down to Texas, Fort Sam Houston in San Antonio.

There is a lot of Mexicans down there in Texas. My buddy and myself went down town one night to one of these what they called a "canteena". The next thing a guy asks, "Are you British?" pointing to us. They don't like the British down there at all. "No", I said, "we're Irish" and laughed. "Oh, you're Irish. We like the Irish". So out with the Tequila and away drinking with us. St. Patrick's day was the next day and he asked us to come down again and so we did and the San Antonio River was dyed green for St. Paddy's Day. The Mexicans really like the Irish over there.

I remember when I was at basic training we had to carry a field pack, about seventy pounds of stuff, rifle and all and we had to climb this mountain, Mount Agony. I don't know why. But only about six of us made it back out of the whole outfit. We had just walked about twenty-four miles and the captain says, "we will be going on a fifteen mile hike. All hands up, all hands up". Nobody put their hands up!

I was there in Texas for two months for my medical training and then I went back to Colorado. From there they sent me up to Pennsylvania for about two months. There were Quakers in that part of the country where I was. And we often went through the area and they were very nice people, very quiet and they would come out on a very hot day to give iced lemonade to you. And you'd see the houses and the buggies and all and think you're back in Ireland!

I was only two months there but about twenty months altogether in the army and then I came back to New York and spent another year at the green houses. Eventually the boss was winding up and she was letting everybody go. It was supposed to be last in first out. She was letting all the old guys go and she was keeping me and I said that that it wasn't right because most of those guys had trained me. But I left there then and I went working for a shipping company, Kilamue Shipping, shipping drugs to different hospitals and institutions, and I stayed there for about two years.

I came back to Ireland in 1969 for about two months on holiday. There were four of us, and we rented out bicycles from Paddy Scanlon on Maiden Street, Lord have mercy on him, who had a bicycle and motor bike shop down there. The first place we cycled was back to Abbeyfeale. But I got up next morning and I could hardly move!

I went back then in September and got another job in another drugs company for a year. They wanted to expand but the people in this village wouldn't let them, they got a concession from the government to move down to North Carolina, making different pills. It was one of the best companies that you could ever work for. They were great people to work for and the workers all had houses that the company gave them. They were there for years and but a lot of the workers got real sour and they started to sabotage all the equipment by putting it into the river, and the company wound up.

So after that I got a job with my brother Timmy, working for a moving company down in the Bronx. After that I got a job in the postal service and was there for about twelve years. That was a good job, sorting mail, magazines, letters, etc. In the village I worked in, the post office would be something like the one in town here and it had two mailmen. The wages and the benefits were very good as it was a government job.

After the twelve years there I decided to come back to Ireland, back in 1981. On my return, I was doing a bit of landscaping and gardening, and I did a lot of graves for people. I went on a FÁS scheme then in 1987.

Back when I was young, people had it very tough but they were happy though. My mother always fed us well and we always had enough to eat, and good clothing. We used get a lot of packages from America and England. If a person is not fed well when they are young, later in life they will get sick.

I often remember, down in my grandmother and my grandfather's house, there were always card games going on. We played '41' for pennies and ha'pennies and told ghost stories, about the headless horseman coming up through Maiden Street and the haunted place back there in Cullinagh with a coach going in and out a passage with police and nuns on it.

We didn't have electricity until the 1950's and we had to pay for the poles. We had no running water at that time either. A fellow would come up from the creamery with a five gallon tank of water and that would do us.

We had a river running through our land and all the kids would swim in it in the summer time. They would go back to our part of the river and they would build up a big weir to block the water to form a pool. I also remember picking mushrooms in the autumn and that was a great pastime long ago. At school there was a handball alley and we also played a small bit of marbles. Then, about October or November, the conkers came and we played with them. I don't see the kids nowadays doing it. I would follow the hurling and football but I was never that good at it but I enjoyed it all the same.

When we made our First Communion, Joe O'Shea took all the class down to North Quay to the hotel there, Curtin's Hotel, and took us all in for breakfast and oranges and apples. We all came out stuffed. It was flogging rain too and I will never forget the drenching we got.

I'm not saying it's true of all kids now, but I think some are spoiled by their parents. Too much money is one thing. There wasn't much money long ago and if you had the price of the pictures two or three times a week you were very lucky.

Newcastle a great town today. But my advice to you is that if you go to America, go there legally. Have your green card or your visa. If you go the other way they will exploit you. They'll give you work but they won't give you the right amount of money. Why would they, when they don't have to. You could always take a chance, but if you're going, go young.

Education and computers, like I said, are making the world go around now, and in years to come there will be hardly any manual work being done. There will be robots running around doing it all for us.

*Huge headlines in **January 1959** in Limerick newspapers announced that Oil was found in Kilkee. Good times ahead!*

***February 1981**, forty-eight youngsters died when fire sweeps through the Star Dust nightclub.*

Eileen Kennelly

My name is Eileen Kennelly and I was born on the 12th February, 1930, in Broadford, Co. Limerick. It is a long time ago now, but it was a thatched house with only two rooms and a kitchen I was born into. There was five of us there; my father and mother, Lord to mercy on them, four girls and a boy. They must have found it hard to raise a family back in those days because there was no money there.

My mother, Lord to mercy on her, worked in Geary's for the lady and she had no bicycle. She used to go home to Newmarket walking and she'd have to be down the following morning again.

My father was a postman all his life. He had a long route on a bicycle, and of course, Christmas Eve you would be lucky if you saw him at 8.00 p.m. But he had a long route! He fell off a bicycle some place, drunk of course, and he went no more then. He enjoyed every bit of it because he'd be meeting everyone. When the travellers would be around Broadford he'd sit down at the end of the road with them talking; "Yerra, they're as good as ourselves," he'd say.

My earliest memory would be of going to school with a friend of mine, bla'guarding and pinching people. There was a girl who used to always tell the teacher what we would be doing, so we used to have a big needle and we'd put it down on the seat and when she sat down she got a pinch. We also used to be fighting with her coming home from school, and then another day we put down this thing that she'd stick to the seat so she couldn't get up. Oh devilment like that! I was always in the corner because I'd be the troublemaker. Like my daughter, I suppose. School days were awful tough too. You'd get the stick every minute you wanted it, across the back or the hands. I liked the poetry but I did nothing and at sums I was useless. Of course, as the teacher used to say, if I put myself to it... They were happy memories.

I also remember a man coming to our house and we were small at that time. They couldn't put us to bed, so he used always call to our house. Well, he'd rise the hair out of your head, telling us stories and how he saw this fella coming down the road and he running and he with no head on him! Oh God almighty, we'd go to bed and we wouldn't sleep at all. Every night he had a ghost story for us. He was great but he's dead since, the Lord have mercy on him.

We hadn't much at home and the money was scarce because that time my father wasn't getting much from the post. So I said I'd stop school at eleven years of age, and every penny I got I took it in home to them because the suit of clothes my father had, they were nearly falling off him, and I said that I wouldn't have my father that way at all. So I went out working with a farmer.

I was working in this house that was very mean with the grub: a small piece of butter between three of us in a side plate. There was a servant boy with me working there and if the woman of the house put big plonks of fat meat with pig's teats in it up to him, he'd eat it! Think that I'd eat that? I often fired it back at her!

Then, when it came on to the pigs, she used to thump me in the back to get me working. One evening, I was throwing this stuff in to the pigs and I stepped aside as she was about to hit me and I hit her one flake into the face and turned her clean upside down into the pigs' trough. When it came to the cow time we used have to go down a couple of miles to milk the cows on the donkey and car and the boys would be gone down on the bicycles before me. Another day, she was coming on with the donkey and car and I hit the donkey a flake and off it went! She was an awful so-and-so.

The hardest time of the year was the hay. I used never like it. If it was a hay day, you'd have to go out and do the hay with them, and come in and eat the dinner and then off out again. It might be seven or eight o'clock when the cows would be going in and you had to milk them then and go out again while it was bright. I used to go up with my missus to her brother's place, which had no boy, and there was no pike fork that time and you'd have to fork it all up with your hands. So I was sick for two or three days with my hands and I said I'd do no more of it.

After that I went to another farmer who was stone blind and my job there was running after cattle around the mountain. I never liked it and when it came to pig-killing this day, they had a pig up on the table to kill and I don't know what aping he was doing, but he just stuck the pig and it ran off down the field. I ran away but he wanted us to go down for the pig. It was all dirt and I wouldn't eat that meat anyway. So I didn't stay there long either as I was getting fed up of it.

I was with an old lady then and she had three cows. She wouldn't leave you milk them alone so she'd be sitting down on one side and you'd be sitting down on the other side and you'd be holding the saucepan for her to milk into it. I didn't stay there either because when she'd be going down to the town or anything she'd put the grub outside the door for you to eat it so you wouldn't be going into the house or anything.

My working day on the farms was usually the same, but when they'd be going to the fair you'd be up at about 1.30am and you'd have to have all the cattle ready. You'd nearly have to go halfway to Dromcolliher with them, and if there was a gap open they were gone and you'd have to follow them. Back to the house then in the dark and you'd have to go down the fields and bring the cows in, milk seven or eight of them and it would still be pitch dark. You'd get nothing to eat until you had the cows milked.

Oh, the cows would go in early in the morning but no thinking about putting them in, in the evening. It would be six or half past six and you'd have to wash the buckets then and leave out the cows and carry them off down the fields, feed calves and go up then and eat your supper.

After supper, I'd often go to bed as I'd be tired. I never saw days off. You nearly worked a week before they'd give you a day off, if you'd ask for it! You'd be working Holy days and Sundays and all and nothing extra for it.

The neighbours helped you out at times, but it all depended on what way the weather was. They might have to do their own work. Drawing in the turf, merciful hour, I hated going back to the bog. I used go back and they used be stripping the turf. I had to take back the scraws and when they'd be throwing back the turf, I'd have to spread it and foot it. I would be cursing it at times. Later, you'd have to draw that home and throw it into the shed and clamp it.

When I was about seventeen, I left all that and I swore that if I had a daughter, she'd go to no farmers. I got a job at the Regional Hospital in Limerick and there I stayed for fifteen months and I got married out of it. I started cleaning, washing ware and taking up the dinners. We had no patients to lift or anything. The wages when I was there weren't so big at all, but now they are. You'd get your wages on a Monday night and you'd have to queue up for it. I lived inside the Regional and so much was kept out of my pay for that.

Sister Gregory, my boss, was lovely. But I remember one morning being sent down with a girl to clean the mortuary. Oh, I wouldn't go to see death at all. I was talking away to her and when I looked back she was gone and the corpse was there! Off up the corridor with me flying. I'd be afraid of my life. Sister Gregory said, "What?" "I'm not going down there no more" says I. "Get in there to the kitchen," she said. I wasn't two minutes there inside the kitchen when I was sent back up the wards again. I'd be afraid of my life of the dead, even yet.

Where I was up in the bog, and it would be five or six miles from where I was living in Broadford, I had little or no contact with friends or with other young girls in the area. I'd see my parents every Sunday at mass and when I'd go home from mass I'd take off my clothes and off up the mountain looking for cattle. So, when I shoved down a small bit, it was then that I had friends but it was lonely at times.

To tell you the truth, we usen't be left out when we were young. We wouldn't get the money to go any place. We'd be lucky to get a ha'penny of a Saturday and that was a lot at that time.

Dance halls were a big thing. We'd go to Ashford or Raheenagh, and we might go to Dromcolliher or away up to Tullylease. Tullylease was a great place to go to the dance then. We'd be asked at home, "what kept you?" "We got tired when we sat down on the floor!" we'd say. I'd go to dances now all right but just to hear the bands. I wouldn't be able to dance.

The Pattern Day was always a big day in the year and another great day was when mass was said in the house, or the stations, as it was called. It was beautiful. You'd be killed from preparing for it but it was worth it because it was a night and a day dancing. Mass would be said and the priest would get his meals and, Bob's your uncle! Clear it away and give us the floor. If you saw us the following day trying to go out and milk the cows and that night again to finish up oh, 'twas great. That's another custom that has died.

Halloween was great sport. We'd have a big basin of water in the middle of the floor and a penny or something inside it, trying to get it. You'd be drowned to the skin, and an apple hanging off the ceiling trying to catch it, but I wouldn't catch a fly.

My mother wouldn't start killing the geese or turkeys until Christmas Eve, and plucking them then. And then cooking them in an open fire, that time in a bastible. You'd be half starved before the turkey would be done. So I don't give in at all to Christmas, God forgive me, as you see there's only two of us there now, my daughter and myself.

On Christmas Eve you'd see them all coming from town with their ponies and cars, carrying their messages and you might see one carrying an old turkey in the back of the car and that was great. They'd be awful drinking there and roaring and shouting - you'd have to lock the door because if they came in they'd fall asleep and you couldn't put them out.

We'd go to midnight mass and come home then and have a cup of tea. I think we usen't go to bed at all, playing around and seeing what we would get, biscuits or something. We'd be lucky if we got a pair of socks from Santa Claus. Christmas day was lonely sometimes. No one could visit you, and that time there were supposed to be no cars on the road but now, in later years, there's cars and there's visitors.

On St. Stephen's Day we had Wren boys and they used to come in and stepdance and we'd make tea for them and have great fun following them. There were people living beside us and for about a fortnight or three weeks before Christmas, that was the music for you. They were playing every hour and every minute, tambourines and every whole thing and their father, Lord have mercy on him, used to get dressed up and we had great sport, but there's none of that now. It was a popular tradition at the time.

We made the St Bridget's cross for the 1st of February. My mother went to mass in the mornings and she was blind and deaf. The priest used always tell her to stay inside but no, she wouldn't stay inside and she'd go by the wall to get there.

Lent was a time of preparation. They say that you should fast, but I never fasted because we were too young, we didn't know what fasting was. We still don't fast but they tell me that I needn't fast now as I'm over seventy. On Easter Sunday my mother would have another turkey and my father, Lord have mercy on him, would bring an Easter egg and halve that between us.

After the Regional, in 1970, I got married but we were only together eight or nine years when he died. He had cancer and I had three children buried in that time. It was very hard and I had an old woman in the house then with me, his mother, and she was awful cantankerous. She wouldn't do anything for you! But we used get on all right sometimes.

It was an unlucky creamery there in Broadford. There was a Cotter man working there long ago and he went over and was caught in one of the big belts going around and he was gutted asunder; there was pieces of him everywhere! There was another man then going around, Mike Hartigan, and he was collecting the small bottles of milk, I don't know what were they for, but then one day he was inside the office getting something, and a rat went up his trousers and out his collar!

There's a lot of them now dead that were working in the creamery but that's shut down now, there's nothing at all left there . There was lovely butter at the creamery. It was lovely and white. And you'd get the back milk that was lovely for baking bread. You'd also get flour and meal and anything there you wanted, briquettes or anything like that. The milk used to go from Broadford up to Mallow and you get lovely chocolate there that my cousin used bring it down to us. That's all gone now.

We had the ration books during World War Two. I think I have a couple of them at home yet. You'd take your rations book and a leaf would be taken out of it for the sugar and tea too - and the small little bit you'd get! We weren't allowed much. But the tea we used to drink and the sugar, we used to spare that for father. My father was a fright for sugar. Four spoons of it and we used have those saccharine tablets. I don't know how we aren't rotten after them. I had an uncle down in Galway who had a shop, and the tea was getting very scarce, so he said he'd send it on to us. He used to send us a big tea chest full of tea and a tea chest full of sugar as well! How we weren't caught, I don't know. It was all the black market then.

There were many characters in the Broadford area and they'd always come in to Newman's, the drunkards that they were, and sit down and sleep. We were noted for drunkards at home. They used always come to our house and we'd never clear them and they'd lie down on the floor and snore. Oh, merciful hour they were a fright!

It is in agriculture that I've seen the greatest changes since the days I lived in Broadford and up to today. What I find is that they have everything, even a thing for making the hay and bringing it in and they have things for cutting the turf and they have milking machines. There was none of those in my time. The biggest change in people is that the old stock are gone and the new ones, well, they don't know if it's on their head or backside they're walking!

*68,000 letters and 17,500 parcels from America are destined for Clare, Tipperary and Limerick were received in one post on the **20th December 1930**.*

*In **May 1970**, Irish Ministers Charlie Haughey and Niall Blaney are charged with procuring arms for the IRA. Blaney's charges are dropped; Haughey is acquitted.*

Frank Dennison

Frank Dennison is currently working for Limerick County Fire Services. He is one of a family of four and has a menswear shop in Abbeyfeale which was established in 1922. He is married to Ann Marie Nolan from Tournafulla. They have six children.

His father Danny was a tailor and his grandfather Jamesie, a weaver. To the best of Frank's knowledge, there were several tailoring establishments in Abbeyfeale in 1955 and the Dennison's were just one of those. These were John Heavy, Sean Broderick, Mike Harnett, Jacques Collins, Johnny Daly, Jim Fitzgerald, Maurice Fitzgerald and the Dennison's - Jamesie and Danny with Billa Wall.

Jamesie Dennison, Frank's grandfather, was a weaver in Abbeyfeale in 1922 and Frank's father, Danny, trained Frank himself to be a tailor. Billa Wall had a long history as a tailor in Abbeyfeale and he worked for and was an extended member of the Dennison family for sixty years.

Frank recalls everyone, the poor and the wealthy, had suits made. There was no class distinction except the frequency of purchase. It cost 2/6 (two shillings and six pence), twelve and a halfpence in today's money, in 1920 to make a suit. That was equivalent to a quarter of the weekly old age pension. In more recent times, it would cost approximately £250 to make a suit.

It took twenty hours to make a suit, from the time the measurements were made to the sewing in of the last button. The material used was a 'worsted' cloth with a high content of wool. Several companies in Dublin, Cork, and

Limerick supplied this material.

The tools used in the trade were a sewing machine for stitching, scissors (pinking shears) for cutting the cloth, chalk for marking the cloth, needle and thread for stitching, an ironing board, a square, and pressing cloth and water to give it a final shape, and of course, patterns to suit all.

People generally had suits made for weddings, Easter, and Confirmation. The custom at that time was that a new suit would not be worn before Easter Sunday. Initially the suit was a Sunday suit but after a period, depending on the wealth of a person, it became an everyday suit.

Frank says that the best customers were the farmers and labourers and that the bank officials generally went to the city to get their clothes made.

In Frank's opinion, tailoring went into decline in Abbeyfeale in the 1960's when ready-made suits became available. Dennisons made their last suit around 1990. Characters like Billa Wall who gave so many years to the trade have now passed on. Frank's father has also passed away and tailoring, like the many other trades and crafts such as the cooper and the shoemaker, have also died out.

However, this was not always the case. According to information gathered by the 1938 School's Project of the Folklore Commission of Ireland, tailors and their trade were to be found throughout the West Limerick area. In Abbeyfeale in the Thirties, flax was grown around the region. It was set in plots like wheat, and when the blue flower would appear on it, it would be pulled and then bogged in a marshy place. It used to be bogged near a well called 'Peter's Well' in County Kerry, and on the banks of the Feale, near Mountcollins creamery bridge. In those times, it had to be bogged very quietly because if the police knew about it, the people would be fined heavily because the water from the flax would poison the river.

When the flax was dry, they used to make sheaves out of it, bring it home and dry it by the fire. They used cloving tongs then to close it. They would hackle it with a hackle and fine clove it again. They used to make thread out of it, both coarse and fine. It would then be taken to the weaver to make cloth out of it. That was the way shirts and sheets were made at that time.

This project also found that in Askeaton, in 1886,there were three tailors and one dressmaker. The tailors were John Collins, Patrick Collins and Timothy Kenny. The dressmaker was Margaret Collins. Similarly, Ballingarry was well served by these industrious tradesmen. The local tailor was Harry Kiely, Turret Street, Ballingarry. He died in 1936 and he worked on his own. The types of materials that he used were Pilate, tweeds and serge. Shirts were often made in the home. Some were made by machine, but generally, all the work was done by hand. The most popular materials used in the making of shirts would have been flannelette, grey wool, calico and plaid. Around the 1900's, flax was grown locally. Shirts were made from the flax, the shirts were called 'Bandle cloth shirts'. The flax was spun, woven, warped and made into cloth. Stockings and socks were made locally, as there was a spinning wheel in almost every farmer's house in the locality. There was also a travelling tailor in Ballingarry who went from house to house making clothes.

There was neither a tailor nor a dressmaker in or near the village of Ballyhahill in 1936. Many ready-made clothes of all kinds were picked up cheaply in the local shops. Many mothers were very handy with the needle, and they could make nearly all their children's clothes at home. Some mothers did a lot of knitting for the family, although home-made socks and stockings were too clumsy and thick to be popular.

Girls on their First Holy Communion always dressed in white on that great occasion, on their heads they wore white veils, and they each held a lighted candle surrounded by flowers while at the altar rails. Girls also dressed in white, with flowing veils of white, on their Confirmation day. At the death of a near relative people used always dress in black for a whole year. By the 1930's, only near relatives wore black and only for a short period.

In Ballyloughnaan, there was no tailor in the district in the 1930's but there was one in Carrigkerry whose name was Griffin. There were lots of tailors in Newcastle West also. They all worked in their homes, but in previous years tailors used to travel around from house to house working. The cloth they worked with was not spun or woven locally. The clothes worn by the local people were all made by the tailor in the locality.

There was no tailor in Feenagh in the 1930's but there was a draper and a dressmaker who supplied much of the clothes needed. Shirts, socks, stockings, trousers and dresses were made locally in the houses and the material was bought in the draper shops. There was no spinning wheels left in the area by 1936.

So well respected and known was the craft of the tailor that his presence is scattered throughout our local folklore. Here are just a few examples, again taken from the 1938 Schools Project.

"Long ago it was an old custom for tailors to go around the houses of those who wanted suits made. A tailor was at a farmer's house one day, and the owner went out milking cows, and a neighbouring woman came in and asked for a coal to light her fire. The tailor told her to take it and she carried it away with her. She was not gone far when the tailor took another coal and put it into a tub of water at the end of the house. He went in to work again and the woman came and asked for another. The tailor gave it to her and he did the same thing again. It quenched and she came back for another, and the tailor did the same thing and it quenched again, and she came back no more.

After a while the woman of the house came in, she began churning cream to make butter. She was churning for a quarter of an hour and no change came on the cream. She asked the tailor what was the matter and he told her to go out to the end of the house were the tub of water was and she would find three pieces of butter in it. She went out and found the three pieces of butter there."

"On a May morning a certain tailor was at a country house and he noticed the woman very uneasy. After a time he watched her, and when she thought he was not looking, she went to a press and got some oil and rubbed it to her hands and legs and she went out the door in the form of a hare. The tailor was watching all the time, and when the 'hare' went out, the tailor went to the press and did the same as the woman. He became a hare the same as the woman, and he followed her until she came to a field where there were many more hares. There was a man on horseback and he said to the hares. "There is one stranger amongst you today" and with that, he hit the tailor that was in the form of a hare with his whip. Then all the hares departed. At that, the tailor did not know what to do and how to get back to his own form again. He followed the woman all the time. The woman went into the house, and she rubbed a horn to herself and she was changed into her own form again. The tailor did the same, when he undressed that night there was a big red and blue mark on his body."

1922: The provisional Free State government orders the first of seventy-seven executions of Anti-Treaty prisioners.

April 1990 and a minor earthquake is felt along the East coast of Ireland.

George Fitzgibbon

George Fitzgibbon is my name, currently living at St. Anne's Nursing Home Dromcolliher, Co. Limerick. I was born in Milford, Co. Cork in the year 1921. There were nine of us in the family. My father was a postman and my mother died at the age of fifty-seven in 1935.

I went to Milford National School until I was fifteen years of age and I hated every moment of it. I thought it the worst time of my life, and I saw some rough times! There were two sisters and two brothers going to school with me at the same time. You had to do every subject and the most important thing of all was Irish. We had to learn everything and speak to each other, even to the teacher, through Irish. Tadhg Shea, our teacher, was strict as far as the Irish language and the Irish games were concerned.

I walked to school as it was within walking distance and I ran home every lunchtime. We only got a half an hour for lunch so I would have to stand at the table and gulp down my food and run back again for the roll call in half an hour. I left Milford National school at the age of fifteen and I went to Charelville Christian Brothers until I was nineteen.

There was no job to spare in Milford of any description after I left school so I joined the Irish Army in 1940. I liked it there to a certain extent, because I am a bit of a disciplinarian and I like discipline. When the *reveille* used to go off at six-thirty in the morning I was one of the first out of bed, and the same thing again when the lights went out at eleven at night. There were one hundred and twenty-one of us in my company and we had to be in the square at a quarter to seven for our call. The Duty Sergeant would then call the roll and then we were put back to barracks. The first thing we had to do was to tidy it up and you tidied up the room and the clothes and made sure that it was spic and span. It was the Duty Officer of the day that used to go around and inspect it, and did so continuously during the day.

Our wage was two shillings a day, which was considered very good at the time because we were all found for. That was a seven day a week job and if you were near enough to it, you were allowed home every night.

Religion in the Army was a big thing because there was a church parade every Sunday morning, headed by the Commanding Officer. If you didn't have a church in the barracks you used the civilian church outside, and that was about a mile away. The people used to adore it and there was a band leading the parade with about seven hundred people in it.

We celebrated Lent, Ash Wednesday, and Good Friday through Irish and there was no meat on Ash Wednesday or Good Friday. We celebrated St. Patrick's Day the same way as today, with a parade and a band, except that it was during the War.

Christmas was very good in so far as our commanding officer, who became General Commanding Officer of the Army later in life, General McKeon, was a good man. I remember meeting him on Christmas Day walking through the village of Castleconnell and he said "Here Fitzgibbon. Why is there nothing going on in the sergeant's place?" "Good God," I said "where do you think we would get the money for that? We don't have a ha'penny in the kitty!" Then he said "Right. You go down to the Shannon Hotel and get two barrels of Guinness, one bottle of whiskey and one bottle of gin and tell Mrs. Keane that I want the mixtures put in free of charge." So I did and we had a great time that Christmas.

I remained in the army until my time was finished and then I was living on my subsidies for a while. I went over to my brother in England and I did nothing for about twelve months until the Second War was over. Then I joined the British Airforce because I thought that I might get the chance of flying, but I didn't because I was unfit and a little bit too old to start learning. You had to volunteer for the airforce and all the volunteers were ex-army men like myself and they were all conned into thinking that there was no problem in getting in. Instead of that, we were told to go back to St. John's Wood and wait there until you were called and I could still be there today after fifty years waiting to be called.

When I was younger, I heard them talking about the Great Famine and how the people suffered an awful lot. All the grain that was coming into Cork Harbor at the time, and the man in charge refused to unload it, so it was all shipped back to England again. That, they said, was the cause of the Famine, because the people had nothing to eat. It lasted three and a half to four years because of the potatoes failing.

I do remember when I saw the first television. I was visiting my in-laws after I was married. We were near each other and so we used to call in, especially when we had the children, and have a cup of tea and cake sometimes. I remember seeing a film on television one day but I thought it was childish so we didn't bother with it at all. It was all advertisements.

I liked travelling, and I spent about fifteen months in India. It was quite good and the people were very nice and the food was excellent. I also spent fifteen months in Malaya before I came back home again.

While I was in the Army I got married and had two children, a boy and a girl. The girl is over in England and the boy is in Spain. He is a dead keen golfer and both he and his wife have cars and they are both quite comfortable. A change from my time.

In all my time travelling and of all the foods I have tasted, I would prefer a feed of cabbage, bacon and potatoes to any roast or whatever they put up before a King or Queen.

1921: An ambush by the IRA outside of Dromkeen, Co. Limerick, results in the deaths of six RIC men and five Black and Tans.

*Two Irishmen, Peter Barnes and James McCormack, are executed for their part in the Coventry bombing of **August 1939.***

Jackie Lenihan

My name is Jackie Lenihan now living in Tournafulla but formally of Caherlevoy, Mountcollins, Co. Limerick. I was born on the 10th January 1911. I have one brother and one sister living, and my parents were small farmers with ten or eleven cows.

I can remember the house I was born in well. It was one of the old farmhouses with a big kitchen and two bedrooms. In the kitchen there was a settle bed and you would think it was an article of furniture. It could be opened up at night for use as a bed and the last place I saw a settle bed like it was in Bunratty castle.

There was a meat barrel at the end of the bed where you'd put in a pig when she'd be killed. She'd be salted and put in there for three weeks until the meat was cured, and there was a meat stick up over us with crooks on it and you'd see the pieces of bacon hung off of them. There was an oven on the fire, usually with a cake of bread inside in it.

I went to school in Mountcollins National School around 1915 at the age of four and I remember everything about my school days. At that time there was roughly about one hundred and twenty boys and there was ninety girls. It was in two parts, a boy's side and a girl's side. We had to work hard going to school and the master was strict and hard, but great. He was a great teacher because he was very dedicated and he always said catechism was the most important lesson of the day, with the result that we had to learn off our catechism by heart.

There was a poem then that we had to learn with two hundred and forty lines in it. It was written by Oliver Goldsmith and was called "The Deserted Village", and you'd have ten lines of that to learn every night and if you didn't, your hands, your "beautiful pieces" as they used to say, wouldn't be "beautiful pieces" anymore. I'll just quote some of it to you;

Sweet Auburn! Loveliest village of the plain,
Where health and plenty cheered the labouring swain,
Where smiling spring its earliest visit paid,
And parting summer's lingering blooms delayed,
Dear lovely bowers of innocence and ease,
Seats of my youth when every sport could please,
How often have I paused on every charm,
The sheltered cot the cultivated farm,
The never-failing brook, the busy mill,
The descent church that topped the neighbouring hill,
The hawthorn bush, that sits beneath the shade,
For talking age and whispering lovers made...

and there is another part of that poem now which is coming to pass;

And trembling shrinking from the spoiler's hand
Far, far away thy children leave the land
I'll fares the land to hastening ills a prey
Where wealth accumulates and men decay
Princes and Lords may flourish or may fade
A breath can make them, as a breath has made;
But a bold peasantry, their countries pride
When once destroyed can never be supplied...

Of course when I was going to school that time it was all through English. There was no Irish when I went in. I'd say I was nearly gone into the sixth class when Irish came in, and the history book we had, I'll always remember it, it was "A Short Review of British History". That would be around 1918 or 1919. It read "The British Empire has a quarter of the land of the globe and a quarter of the people in it". It was said the sun would never set on her dominions and we learned all about England. We learned a bit about Ireland but it was mostly England and Scotland and the Master that was teaching us said the Irish had completely ruined the education system.

We walked to school in Mountcollins. There was a townland in the parish of Rockchapel called Meeng and all the children came across the fields from there. Meeng is at the boundaries of the three counties, Cork, Kerry and Limerick, and at that time there was no bridge crossing from Limerick to Cork, only a foot bridge, and it seems it was carried by the flood, but all the children in the twenty-two houses in Meeng came to Mountcollins school. It was a long journey across the fields.

I left school at the age of thirteen. Very few people went to secondary school in my time because there was no secondary school around. There was none in Abbeyfeale and the nearest after that would be Listowel. It was eight pounds a year for a day student. A few of them went to Listowel, others went to America and some of them went into service and went to the hiring fair in Newcastle, where they might stay around with farmers in the mountains first, but the wages would be better in the county. The hiring fair in Newcastle would be on a Thursday, from the middle of January up to St. Patrick's day.

My first job was at home, working on the small farm. The week's work would vary but I'd be up at six o' clock at the latest and it was one hard day. In every farm in those days there was a limekiln for burning lime. The nearest limestone quarry to us in Caherlevoy was Taur, at the other side of Newmarket. I might be called in the morning at five o' clock to tackle my horse, get my dinner and go on to Taur, eleven miles away, and put out six or seven ton of limestone from the quarry on the side of the public road.

Then you'd have to square your heap of limestone. It might be seven or eight feet long, four or five feet wide and about three feet high, and there would be a man from the quarry there and he'd come along and tape it at so much a ton. He'd know how many tons would be in your heap of limestone when it would be squared. We'd bring that home and it would be burned in a limekiln and would be thrown out on the land, most of it mountain, to cultivate it.

I'll tell you now about income. The man over across the way had a boy with him and he told me it was eleven pounds he was getting for the eleven months. That would be about five shillings a week. It was going up then, but at that time, a lad of sixteen might be getting twenty pounds. The top wages that time would be around thirty pounds for eleven months. If a man was able to follow horses and do ploughing and mowing he might get thirty-five pounds.

At the hiring fair in Newcastle, a boy had to be able to milk ten cows morning and evening and a girl had to milk eight. They wouldn't see home until Christmas Eve from the 1st February. There were no bicycles that time or anything. I know people that were there and I know where they were housed and I know several boys and girls from Mountcollins who went to the hiring fair in Newcastle and were hired over the country. I'll tell you one story about a certain family who were small farmers and I think there were four girls in it. The father would tackle the horse and he'd put the girls in the car and land them at the hiring fair in Newcastle and they'd be hired by farmers as far away as Charleville. But his two sons were intelligent and they were put into Mungret College, which at that time, for a boarder, was forty-five pounds a year, paid for with the girls' wages. And when the boys would come home on holidays at the beginning of June, they'd be put working for a farmer in County Limerick until they went back in September. Those two boys became priests and one of them was a Doctor of Divinity when he was ordained.

When we were making butter there were three farmers; our next-door neighbours and a woman about a field over from the house, that joined in butter making. At that time there was a dairy attached to every house. It was a thatched building, kept very well whitewashed and plastered on the inside and the barrel was inside there for churning the butter and also the cream.

The railway back then was going from Limerick and there was a man by the name of Murphy from Mountcollins parish who was a butter merchant in Dublin. He would buy the butter and it would be put on rail at Devon Road in a special butter wagon to Dublin. The price of your butter would come down to you then by post and I think the empty boxes used to come back as well. The firkins held the butter, and it was the coopers that made them, with the result that coopering was a very popular trade. There was two or three keeping the farmers supplied with firkins. I know when the firkin was made, it was going to the butter market in Cork. My grandfather used to talk about the going to Cork. They'd start after the dinner with a horse and go as far as Kanturk, and they had some other place to stay then outside Cork, Átha na Loinsigh, and they'd go into Cork then and they'd bring back a bag load of things for the local shopkeepers.

People used to grow their own vegetables and they would have big gardens of spuds set, up to a statute acre at any time, and that used be done by hand as there was plenty of labour around at that time. The servant boys, before they'd go out the first of February, might have gardens of *taobhóids*, lazy beds or ridges, and they'd turn them at so much a quarter or at so much a half acre.

Of course, it was all the spade and the scythe in those days. Cutting hay was with the scythe, and all the meadows were marked, and a day's work for a man was roughly a statute acre. Hard work, but they took no notice of it. When the harvest would start there might be three or four of you going, cutting hay and going to the house in the morning for your breakfast. You'd wait until it would be a clear day and you'd work for two hours before you'd be called to the breakfast. For feeding the mowers in those days there was, "baker's bread" and new milk, which they used to call, "goodie". They'd cut away then and they'd have their task finished for maybe four or five o'clock in the evening.

The creamery in Mountcollins was closed for a while, as there was some dispute. When creameries were first built they belonged to a company, a proprietor, and the farmers bought them out around 1910. There was a parish priest here in Ballycomane in Tournafulla named Fr. Reeves and he was very instrumental in getting the farmers to buy out the Co-op. I remember there was a big notice long ago, "Mountcollins WHC, WJ Stokes General Manager" above the one here.

There were two blacksmiths in Mountcollins. Blacksmiths were very busy in those days and they used to make spades as well as shoeing horses, making gates and banding wheels, but there are none left now.

The blacksmith's work was hard work -
Under a spring chestnut tree, the village smith he stands,
The smith a mighty man is he, with large and sinewy hands,
The muscles of his grainy arms are thick as iron bands,
His hair is crisp, 'tis black, it's long, his face is like a tan,
His brow is wet with honest sweat, he earns what e'er he can,
And looks the whole world in his face, for he owes not e'er a man.

That was one of the poems going to school and it wasn't written by Goldsmith, it was written by Longfellow.

We grew flax ourselves that time. They made these bandle cloth shirts, as they called them. They were very heavy and were probably made at home. There was a lot of tailoring done at home that time and of course, knitting, and they had a woollen mill in Knocknagoshel that time. Blankets and thread they'd make there, and it was the Shaughnessys that had it.

Of course there was a flourmill here beyond Kantogher as well. Dr. Shaughnessy, you see, had it and it was run by the river Banogue.

I remember the games I played and I'll tell you about one of them. I was playing football in Rockchapel against Ballydesmond. The following morning I knew I'd be going out to Taur putting out seven or eight ton of limestone. So on I went anyway and even though I was tired, I had to do so much. There were two quarry men and one of them, what he'd be doing all day, was working with a hand drill and he boring the rock with that drill. They'd come on then and they'd blast it with blasting powder. So anyway, I said to one of the quarry men, "Paddy" says I, "I'm very tired today. I was kicking football at the Rock' yesterday". "Foolish game, Johnny" says he, "following a bag of wind"! He never saw a football in his life, the same man. I was playing football for Mountcollins for a few years and I used to go to the All-Ireland in Dublin, especially when Kerry would be playing. My grandmother came from Kerry, from Duagh.

There were different kinds of entertainment in the olden days and one form was the dancing schools in the wintertime. A dancing school would be held in a house and there would be the dancing master and the musician. He'd come to the house to teach dancing. Grady was a noted musician in the old days before my time; he was known as well as a music teacher. Word came one day to the dancing school that huntsmen were after killing a fox in the wood. So Grady went with the people of the dancing school to where the fox and the huntsmen were and he played "The Fox Chase" over the dead fox and he finished up with another piece of music called "The Fox Hunter's Jig". An old man told me this and he was at the dancing school that day and he'd never forget it - it was a frosty day and he was a fine musician.

There were good storytellers in those days too. The stories I might be telling you now, my grandfather told to me, but they mightn't be all true and I couldn't credit a lot of them.

There were plenty of good characters and there was very little contact in those days with the outside world. There was a man living down from us and he had only three cows, a donkey and a pony, but he used to break bog deal to sell. Bog deal is the timber you'd get in the bog. But he used to give a load of bog deal to the post-mistress and what she was giving him for it was the 'Weekly Cork Examiner', and his son said the neighbours would come round to read it in turn. That will tell you how very little contact there was with the outside world.

The first bicycles that came out were the penny-farthings, which had one big wheel in front and one small wheel behind, and the R.I.C. were the first to get the bicycles. There was a young lad in our part of the country and they were setting turnips one day and the farmer sent him to Abbeyfeale for turnip seed. The young lad came out above at Mountmahon and he was barefoot. Anyway, he saw the R.I.C. man coming on down on the bicycle and he thought it was the Devil riding the wind. He ran for the town as hard as he could and the first shop he met, he threw himself down inside exhausted. So the shopkeeper asked him what was wrong. "The devil is after me and he's riding the wind", says he. The shopkeeper looked out and he saw the R.I.C. passing on the penny-farthing bicycle. It will just tell you how people viewed things back then.

The first car I saw in Mountcollins was when an inspector came to the school and there was a man driving him. That would be around 1920. The first motor car that was in the parish was belonging to Master O'Sullivan who was teaching here in Tournafulla. He was from Kenmare and his wife was another Kerry woman and it cost one hundred and twenty five pounds. It was a two-seater with a canvas hood.

In rural Ireland in those days, it was forbidden to marry from the first

Sunday in Advent until after the Epiphany, and from Ash Wednesday until after Easter Sunday, with the result that most of the rural marriages were during Shrove. From after the 6th January until Shrove Tuesday it would be the season of matchmaking and of course, it was all matchmaking long ago. There was a scale of fortune and any girl wouldn't go into a farm that time with one hand as long as the other at all. It was like this; if you had ten cows, two hundred pounds for the girl that would be going in there. If you had fifteen cows, three hundred pounds and if you had twenty cows, four hundred pounds and so on. That was the scale of matchmaking.

We would do a pile of work before Christmas; stowing things away and having every place nice and tidy outside. We used to prepare a special Christmas dinner for the cows and calves, the cattle and horses. At that time we used to grow turnips. We'd pulp a big tub of turnips for Christmas Day and we'd have about four sheaves of oats to every cow with a big bucket of turnips that would be her Christmas dinner. Of course then there'd be the goose. Geese were very prominent that time and all the weddings would be in houses and it was stuffed geese that were used for the wedding dinner. If there were a few girls in a house you'd notice after Christmas there might be three or four of the geese left up. They'd say "he's getting one of the daughters married".

At the Easter Stations all the names of the family would be called out and there was a day for the defaulters and they'd see that everyone would do their Easter duty. The names would be called out and if you were absent then, you'd have to come back another day. Of course, there were servants in every farmers house that time. The big farmers kept two boys and a girl. A middling sized farmer, he kept a servant boy at least, and a girl of course. Then there was the washer women going round as well, washing clothes but I remember they'd be a different day for each townland. Caherlevoy we'll say would be Wednesday.

My people were evicted from the lower part of Caherlevoy in 1852 and they moved up into the mountain. I heard my grandfather saying the few cattle that they had, you would hardly see them inside in the heather. They had to build mud houses when they were evicted. My grandfather was born in 1845 and the famine came in 1847. At that time nobody owned their own land, it was the landlords that owned it. Caherlevoy belonged to a man, Dunscombe, who lived in Cork. If you ever go through Mountcollins, there is a bridge before you go to the school that's there now, and you'll see written on it, *"erected by Nicholas Dunscombe 1852"*. He made changes then in the land with his tenants. It seems he was a soft-hearted man. He sold it then to the Creagh Harnetts.

The Creagh Harnetts lived in Abbeyfeale at Moynsha. A part of the rent to the Creagh Harnetts was two rails of turf from every tenant to be delivered into Moynsha. But there was very high regard for the Creagh Harnetts. They were very decent people who wouldn't press you for rent. But two horse loads of turf came from every tenant and I think there was about twenty tenants in their Caherlevoy estate. They also came around shooting a lot of game at that time. You had grouse and all different kinds of game.

My grandfather said that only for turnips they would have died at the time of the Famine. It wasn't exactly an eviction that time, they were put into another part of the property, but it was a mountain part, into poor land that was only all heather. There would be two houses together, you know, but in townlands then, where they'd be four of five houses, the people in the farthest up part of the townland would call that place Bunabhaile.

I'll tell you a story about Bunabhaile. The woman in one of the houses said to the husband this night, "will you put the children to bed tonight?" "I will", he said. She was going out. She wasn't going to the local tavern now. Maybe she might be looking for a dozen hatching eggs or the loan of a hatching hen. Maybe a fox killed her gander and she might know someplace where there was an idle gander. But eventually she came back, "Oh, you have them all in bed" she said. "I put eleven of them to bed," he said.

"Sure, we have only ten!" Wasn't he after putting one of the neighbour's children in with them!

I can remember stories about the 1916 rising because the IRA used to stay with us. My mother got up every hour of the night to them but there was a snag at the same time; the names of the people of the house had to be written on the back of the door. That was an order by the police.

I remember the Black & Tan barracks in Mountcollins was raided and the West Limerick IRA, maybe ten or twelve of them, were sent there. I remember coming home from school one evening and there was six of them eating the dinner at our place. That night the barracks was raided and one of the IRA men was wounded. His name was Dan Jerry O'Connor and there was another boy there from Brosna, Davy Cahill, and he went out and pulled him in from wherever he was. He put him on his back and landed him behind inside in a wood where they got the doctor to him and he was saved, but the barrack was never taken, after all that.

I don't remember Fr. Casey but I heard stories of him. I'll tell you now, there was a landlord in Ballaugh, and of course Fr. Casey was up against the landlords and he got their cattle stolen and killed outside in Caherlevoy. The Mountcolllins crowd were involved in the taking of them, and a share from Abbeyfeale. They brought them down across the railway, they brought them up to Caherlevoy and they slaughtered them and buried them in a bog above in Caherlevoy.

The Civil War too was a sad tragedy and caused awful bitterness and everything for Ireland. Michael Collins was a great man and Eamon de Valera was a great man, that's what they used to say about them. It was sad to see brother fighting against brother. It was tragic and there was a lot of bitterness.

The time of the last war, it started in 1939 and everything went scarce, it did. We used to grow our own wheat that time. We used to scratch the wheat with a barrel inside in the house, and pick up the grain and winnow it, and bring it to the mill and they'd take out the pollard or the bran, whatever you liked, but the first thing they'd do was to dry it and 'twas a girl from Abbeyfeale that was in charge of it. Her name was Eily Harnett, I think she was from Ballaugh, over there from near where Dr. Mc Carthy lived. She had some connection with Dr. Shaughnessy. The tea was cut down to an ounce and you had a ration book to claim it. Everyone had a ration book, you see, but I mean to say it wouldn't be enough, especially for working people.

I'm living at this address sixteen years. I was living at the address in Mountcollins since I was born. I met my partner at a dance in Mountcollins. I don't know if the children have an easier or harder time nowadays, but I do think television has them ruined. It is the baby-sitter now. But there is one thing that puzzles me and I can't get over it; how was a big family reared in the old days? It was the grandparents that reared them, I'd say.

People were emigrating by the new time and there used to be an American wake the night before they'd go. There would be a dance at the house where the girl or boy would be going and they might convey them the next day as far as Newmarket or even as far as Queenstown (Cobh) and when the liner would be going out, they'd be playing "The Last Glimpse of Ireland". It was by boat they travelled that time to America and they'd be six or seven days going. But they sent home piles of money, those people. I know one girl, there was thirteen of them in the family, who was sending home eight pounds a month constantly and that was big money that time. They went and went and went and they all did well.

I was talking to a woman years ago that was ninety-six when she came home. Herself and her brother were together in America and at that time in some places in the States there was notices up "No Catholics need apply". She got a job but her brother didn't and she had to keep the brother going for a long time, so it wasn't all smooth sailing for them.

April 1911 *and the greatest ship ever built, the Titanic, is launched in Belfast.*

1920: Lord Mayor of Cork, Tomas MacCurtain, shot dead by crown forces outside his home in Cork.

James Casey

My name is James Casey and I'm living at 73 Assumpta Park, Newcastle West, Co. Limerick. I was born in Rathkeale in 1923 where I lived, grew up and went to school until I was twenty.

My father was a hairdresser and my mother was a housekeeper. But as I say, we all grew up together there and then. But when you were growing up then you made your own entertainment as there was nothing and if you had a six pence, you were a millionaire. But the neighbours were very good around the place and anybody who had gardens, which they did in those days, they'd give you a bag of vegetables and things, which meant a lot to people. People were more united then than they are today. There is a lot of selfishness and jealously around now, but in those days, everybody was the same. You could go away and leave your doors and windows open, which you cannot do now.

All the trades have gone too. They used to say that there was five of everything in Rathkeale. Five of everything; five blacksmiths, five tailors, five bakeries and so on. I think from Church to Abbey there was twenty-four pubs in the town; that was from the top of Church Street at one end up to the Abbey at the other end. That's what they used to say anyway.

I think my mother's dead about ten years and my father's dead for about fifteen years. We lived on the main street there in Rathkeale. It was a marvellous town in those days. There was anything and everything there, but as I said, you wouldn't always have the money for it. You had nice people there, you had good neighbours. If you wanted to get out and about, you could get out and about and you were safe in doing it.

I remember, in the summer time, we used to go down robbing the orchards. We went into a place where this women had a big hole in the wall to get the out and we saw it. We went down the river and we saw it and we thought, "cool, we can get in here". So of course we thought we were bloody clever and we put our jumpers inside our trousers and filled our jumpers with apples. And she followed us but we couldn't get out of the hole in the wall. She had seen us from the kitchen window and she came out and we all went for the hole in the wall, and couldn't come out. And so there were the apples and even cider everywhere!

We used to like going on the trains because it was a novelty too. We used to walk to Ballingarrane and then it was five pence to go to Foynes for the Regatta, and that used to be a great day out for us. Go down there at two in the afternoon and come back at eight in the evening. Then, from Rathkeale to Limerick, I think it was sixpence. You couldn't stand at a bus stop now today for sixpence.

We had an awful habit of going around putting a reel of thread on to people's doorknockers and when one would open their door the thread would lift the knocker on the door across the way and they'd be opening the door all night. You made your own fun when you had nothing else. Of course, some people would say you were devious and that but you didn't see it that way, you just took a laugh out of it.

You never got into trouble with the Guards. If you did, it was only for a bit of craic. In those days the Guards were different, they turned around and they used to have a cane, and they'd hit you around the bloody neck with it and they'd say, "I'll tell your father" and that was worse than being summoned. You'd be afraid to go in home in case they would tell your father because you'd be grounded, and you'd be left out no more. Oh God, my parents wouldn't hesitate in giving you a clout if you misbehaved yourself. But I think it stood to you in the end.

The priests and the nuns were tough too. The priests, the Holy fathers, would come around and they'd frighten the life out of you. There was a priest in Rathkeale and he had an Alsatian dog trained that when he went out the road at night, if the dog saw any boy and girl against the wall, he would sit down there until the priest would come along, and he'd hit them and send them home. I'm telling you, they'd frighten the life out of you. Let's face it, they were the commanders of the place, they were running the place, and they had the best of everything.

The school was only up the road from me in Thomas Street, Rathkeale. There were two schools there, what they used to call the Infant school, which was the National boys school, and the Convent, which was the girls school, but now I believe it is all mixed.

I liked secondary school but I didn't like national school. The homework was very tough and if you didn't get it right you were kept in after school to do it. And in those days you wanted to get out as quick as you could but there was no getting away with it. You had to have it done. We used to have inspectors come around to us, examining you and doing this and that, and they'd examine you individually. Then, of course, you went to the secondary school and it was different altogether, it was more free and easy and I think you learned more.

The teachers were very tough and there was no sparing of anything . It was kind of up to yourself to learn it or leave it, but one of the teachers had a big strap and he'd belt you with it. I mean <u>really</u> belt you with it. I remember I got twenty-four slaps one day and my hands swelled up to my arm and I was home for a week with it.

The doctors and nurses used to come out to the school because there was a fever going around at that time but I don't know was it scarlet fever or diphtheria. There were many epidemics in those days because I think people didn't have the nourishment. When you were sick they'd give you a bottle of cod liver oil and shove it back your throat. And you'd be sick after the cod liver oil, worse than the sickness you had before!

I was in national school until I was fourteen and I was at the secondary school for four years, I think. I got my Inter. and Leaving Certs there and I left then, but there was no work about.

Work was very hard to come by. It wasn't what you knew, it was who you knew. I got a job in the Post Office and they said it was temporary. I took it and I was there for twelve months but then of course, they said that they were getting new staff in, so that was it.

The Post Office mistress was all right but she could be a bit edgy at times though. She'd have her good days and her bad days, but you didn't take any notice, she'd give you a shout or something and after that it was all forgotten again. The pay wasn't bad at all. I think it was about one pound or something a week, which wasn't bad for then, and it was a government job.

You had the E.S.B., the Post Office, the telephones, the railways, and you had the buses, the five main jobs in Ireland at the time, if you could get on them.

Then the County Council brought in a work scheme and we went cutting turf back in the bog. But it was all money; you did it for money. You had nothing and work, well, work was only just a word. We were in the bog for a couple of months and there was quite a few of us there from around this area. It only lasted for a while but it was money we were glad to get . Then, when the bog was finished, they started a scheme on the Railway, painting the bridges, and so we got a job there but we walked from Adare right through to Barna and we had to cycle from Rathkeale to Barna every morning and every night. The wage we received was five shillings and six pence.

We were there for a few months and then when that was finished, they kept us on for a another six months, relaying. That was putting down the tracks to complete the contract and I thought, I've had enough, and I packed up and I went over to England.

When I went over there first it was during World War Two and the ration books were out and you were rationed on everything. If you wanted a suit of clothes, your whole book went. Anyway, when you were there you stayed in digs. We went in there one night and we found this lovely smell and said, here goes, there's a great fry up in here. The landlady put this meal in front of us and we thought it was beautiful. It tasted lovely because that time you only got dried eggs, so many ounces of tea, and so many ounces of butter, but it wasn't butter, it was margarine at the time. There was no such thing as jam or sweets, and cigarettes were very scarce. Anyway, she asked us how did we like our dinner. We said beautiful, especially the nice steaks. It was then that she said that they were horsemeat! Yeah, and it tasted beautiful, but we felt sick about it when we'd think about it later! God, it could have all came up again!

It was tough going in England and it was very hard to get digs because of the Irish blokes. They used to get drunk and they'd set fire to the beds from smoking in them, along with everything else inside in the digs. Then, when you were looking for digs, they'd ask if you were Irish and when you'd say you were, they'd say sorry but they couldn't let us stay because the last Irish people that were there set fire to the beds so it was very hard, tough going.

Everybody went to England, you had no choice but to go at the time. I was in London for about three years and I was painting there. I got a good job, it was all around the area, but I got kind of fed up with it. But I got a good job then with Maxfactor, the make-up company, in Bond Street, doing the painting and decorating there. I was there for six years and the money was good.

I used to start at six in the morning and finish at two that afternoon, and then you'd go on shifts. For those, you'd go in at two in the morning and finish at ten, and then you'd go in at ten in the evening and finish at six the next morning. That was an eight-hour day, Monday to Friday, but if you went in on Sunday, you'd get triple time.

My boss was very nice and they were marvellous people to work for, even the owners, who were two brothers. They knew everybody by their names. They'd come up and talk to you and ask you if you had any problems, is everything all right, or is this, that, and the other okay. I was promoted there and I was shifted down to Bournemouth, to their main factory. Bournemouth was a lovely place, a beautiful seaside resort there. I also married and had a daughter while I was down there.

I was transferred to what they used to call maintenance staff, which consisted of the mechanics who used to do the truck repairs, the pipe fitters and the carpenters and so on. We kept the factories going. I was working with them for twenty-one years.

For entertainment at the time it was all dancing and sport. We had a great club at Maxfactor. They had everything you wanted to play. I played rugby for Maxfactor and I played rugby for the school that my daughter went to. They used to class us as the Kingsley Old Boys.

Then I heard they were going to be taken over, which they were, by Procter and Gamble, the people who make the shampoo. They were taken over by them and moved up North. They knocked the factory completely in Bournemouth.

I took retirement then and my wife died and I thought that this was it so I came back to Ireland and I bought this place and I'm here since.

In my younger days, before I went to England, we used to come here to Newcastle, to a lovely dance hall over where the Castle is. There the Nash's had a beautiful dancehall. There was a band from Newcastle headed by Darky Divine and then there Tony Hayes' father, Jackie Hayes, who had a band from Rathkeale. There was a bloke living alongside me, Arthur O'Shea, who had a band, and they used to tour around to different places. They used to go down to the hall in Shanagolden and there was another beautiful hall in Glin, I don't know whether it is still there or not, "The Ocean", and then there was the Deel Hall in Rathkeale.

We used to cycle into Limerick and we'd go into Cruises Hotel, where Cruises Street is now, and there was also the "Stella", which was another dance hall. About five or six of us would cycle in and we'd be coming home at about three in the morning when you wouldn't meet a soul.

I went in one night with a bloke and his car broke down on the way home where the Regional Hospital is now, but it was only a big field at that time. There was a few of us there but none of us knew anything about the car and he only knew how to drive it! We said we'd wait until the bloke bringing the papers came along and we'd ask him to help us out. So he came anyway and we stopped him and he said he couldn't take all of us, but he'd take one of us into Patrickswell but we said no. The four of us said we had better start walking, so off we went.

Along the way, the bloke that owned the car got tired and we picked up a few big sticks and put a big branch of a tree across them and we carried him from Limerick to Adare, changing hands all the time we were walking. We got to the place in Adare where there is a big Cross over a fountain beside the Church and took his shoes and socks off there. We put his feet into the water and Christ, we couldn't get his shoes and socks back on anymore. His feet had swelled up so we still had to carry him along the same way as before. As luck had it, there was a lorry coming anyway so we flagged it down and asked the driver where he was going and he said he was going as far as Rathkeale, so we said we'd go as far as Rathkeale with him.

But sure we never knew that the poor fellow had leukaemia. We could have killed him by putting his feet into the cold water. All up his leg, up as far as his knee, had swelled up but we thought it was from the dancing.

We had good times, although they were poor times, and we enjoyed ourselves. It was a lot easier when there was no violence or there were no drugs. We never thought of drugs; all that we wanted was half a crown to go to the dance. If you had five shillings you were a millionaire because you could get a packet of cigarettes for ten pence, and if you met a girl at the dance you could buy her a bottle of lemonade and you still had change out of five shillings.

There was no television and we had very few radios, as it was only people with a lot of money who had radios. I don't even think you would stay inside to watch television in those days, as you were always out. You were either playing football or swimming, there was always something. You wouldn't be used to what was on, I mean, you would go over and press a button and you got this and you got that and you know, you were in some-body else's house, you were at the races or something. The first television I ever saw was at an exhibition in London. They had a television there, and I might as well be honest, but I didn't know what the hell was going on. I couldn't make out what it was. That was the first television I really ever saw, but, then again, when I came home, a few people had televisions. They were beginning to find their feet, as the saying goes, but television, you can get sick of it. Today it has ruined people's lives. There was a bloke on television there the other night and he showed his arm, and he couldn't get anymore needles into his arm after all the drugs. Oh, it was vile to look at it, but he said he was coming off of it, now he was getting his treatment. He said fifty, sixty, seventy pounds a day he'd spend on the drugs. He stole his mother's wedding ring, and then he stole his father's wedding ring for drugs.

My father told me, though I don't remember it, that we went to see this person that had died and he belonged to the travelling community. They laid him out and they were all kneeling down praying. In those days when they died, they used to dress them the way they were everyday and they used to put all the harnesses of the horses and everything on the bed along-side him. So anyway, they were all sitting inside in the room and all of a sudden he stood up and said, "What in the name of Jesus is wrong with ye? Are ye trying to kill me?" He frightened the life out of the whole lot of them and the house emptied with people going in all directions! He was in a coma, it seems, but they thought he was dead!

We wouldn't believe anything back in those days. You'd hear of these things, this, that, and the other, but you wouldn't take any notice of it, they used to say things but... well, you have to see these things happen to believe them. I was down in a place called Pallaskenry one day. I had an aunt living down there and it was the time they were building the Church in Copsewood and they were holding a carnival there inside the grounds. People used to have goats in those days and they used to have a chain around their neck, with maybe two tied together. I was walking home from the carnival, around midnight, and I walked in between these things and I could feel something squeezing my legs and I put my hand down and I felt this hairy thing and I didn't know what it was. Next, the old goat let a "mahh" out of him.... I didn't have the energy to kick him because he frightened the life out of me. I tell you, I wasn't out late the next night!

My wife and I went to school together here in Ireland and then I met her again when I went over to England. We were going out together for about three years, we came home then and got married here. She was nursing in England, but then she got Multiple Sclerosis and died. She had it for twenty-one years, the misfortune. When she died I thought, that was it. I sold up over in England and I came over here and I am quite happy here now.

It's sad, with the money that's in the country today, it's awfully sad to see the state of some people. I know I saw them over in England, going around homeless at night, when we were in the West End of London. They'd go around there to the Soup Wagon, and they'd give them cups of soup and a lump of bread. Now, it's no better here. That's real poverty, it's like living in a bloody prison. The poor old things are sitting down wrapped up in old boxes and bits of this and that and they go around to all the restaurants pinching stuff out of the dustbin. It just shouldn't be.

1923: The Garda Siochana is established by an act of the Irish Free State, with Eoin O'Duffy as commissioner, in August.

1941: German accidently bomb North Strand in Dublin, killing thirty-four people.

James Fitzsimons

I'm James Fitzsimons from Main Street, Foynes. I was born in Shanagolden, up the old road, on 12/04/1933. My earliest memory is of going to hospital when I broke my hand from a fall from a hay barn. Joe Hartnett was giving out hay to Jerry O'Connor's cows and while he was taking in one lot of the hay didn't I go up the ladder and hide above in it. He took away the ladder when he was finished and I stayed above. I called out to a brother of mine to take me down and he said to sit down and slip down onto his shoulders. But the hay was up under the chute of the barn so when I stepped out and down onto his back, I went out his head and broke my hand. I was taken to St. John's Hospital in Limerick and there was a fever out at that time, diphtheria, and I was put in a fever ward as I suppose they thought there was no hope for me anyway. I hadn't it as bad as the rest of them and I didn't die but it was about three weeks or a month later before they started looking after my hand and so there was a bad job made of it in the end.

We had a bit of land at home and I had a great father and mother who worked very hard for us. There was eight of us there, six boys and two girls.

I remember going to Mass on a horse and trap we had ourselves. They would be all tied above outside the chapel with the bikes, and lots of fellows going to the creamery on a Sunday would drive their donkeys and cars, tie them up and go into mass.

There is one thing that will stick out in my mind when I was going to the bog with my father sixty years ago. On the way there, we passed three little cabins that were thatched with rushes and had little windows with a small tankard for the chimney. They were made of mud and had mud floors. I don't know how many rooms they had but there was seven or eight children in them and as far as I know, there was one cabin there that had thirteen people in it. Today, you can go anywhere in the country and there is beautiful new house for everyone, fit for the king, with only one, two or three children in them and that is a big change.

My brothers, sisters and myself got on fine because our mother and father kept a barrier up with us all the time and you had to do what you were told and no backchat. If you gave a bit of backchat or said you wouldn't do it, you can be sure that whatever they had said to you after, you would do it. Young lads would often fight and they would stick in each other over something and maybe have a few pucks, but there was no such thing as that if the father and mother were around.

At that time there was no way that doing anything the easy way. Everything had to be done the hard way. Hay had to be saved with the pikes and the old horses and the swath turners and you know turf had to be cut with the sleán and spread out in the bog. The cows had to be milked by hand and there were big families everywhere.

I went to the old school at the back of the creamery in Shanagolden when I was five years old. It was a big classroom with lots of garsoons there and a lot of them barefoot, with knitted pullovers and little hand knit socks. There was a forge there across from the school where you would hear the anvil ringing all day long, but that's not there anymore either.

It was very old fashioned and the teachers were very severe, not like today, and there was no communication between them and us. We were in dread of our lives of them and if you didn't know your lessons, they would really hammer you. The standard of education was poor and the system was wrong in my thinking. The average young fellow was all right, but you had

a few garsoons that wouldn't be up to the rest of them and they were murdered, Jesus help us, they used be killed. The teachers were very cruel.

There was huge importance in the First Holy Communion and the
Confirmation and it was catechism all the time when you were due to get
either. The priest was in to examine you once a week in the year of the
Confirmation and he would slap you too if you missed a question. I was at
my grandchildren's Confirmation recently and to see the way they were
brought out, the choir, the teachers and the youngsters. They were all going
up reading their little piece and when it was over then they were all into
cars and off. We went to the Woodlands and there was a good few that went
to the Devon Inn and the Countenay Hotel in Newcastle West. None of that
was there at all in our time. I remember when I got my Confirmation, the
very minute it was over it was home and change your clothes as you were
going no where. So things have improved in that sense.

When you got up in the morning you would have to do so much work
before you went to school and when got home you would have to start
working again before you went to your books and it was off to bed at about
half past nine.

I went on to the Tech in Shanagolden and a great school it was. There were
good teachers there to teach you mechanical drawing and carpentry and a
lot of fellows did well out of that. I went there for two years and I left that
then and I served my time to be a butcher.

I was a butcher for twenty years of my life, five in Limerick, where I served
my time, and fifteen outside in the county. I was an apprentice to Joe Barry
on Harstonge Street and I'll tell you, you had to work hard there. I will
never forget there was a little young lad, Christy, on a messenger bike and
he had no protective clothing or anything, it was just up on the old bike and
away with him. He went out to the City Home with puddings and sausages
and he was outside a long time so when he got back, old Joe Barry called

him, "Christy, come here boy. Where were you till now boy?" And Barry knew well where he was. "I was out side at the City home sir" Christy says. "God blast it", Barry said "I would be out on my knees twice since you left here and you have a bicycle". The young lad was only fourteen years and he was one of twelve in his family and this is a fact and I will never forget this like. The young lad pipes up, "Wouldn't you get a better bicycle than that below in Corkanree?" Corkanree was the dump that time. But I will never forget old Barry saying, "Get your coat boy and go away home. There is only one boss here." So the young lay got his coat anyway and he turned around and looked at old Barry and he like a bear. "There was only one Barry any good and that was Kevin, and he was no relation of yours!" said the lad and he walking out the door.

The first day I started, I will never forget and my father was with me. We had to go down town and get a white coat and we came up and old Barry said to my father, "Mr Fitzsimons, I have to take this boy on a month's trial and he might not want me and I might not want him. I have no business of a fool". He turned and said to me quickly, "You have five years to serve. Your wages will be a pound a week the first year, thirty shillings a week the second year, two pounds a week the third year, three pounds the fourth year and four pounds a week the fifth year. Now, what am I after saying to you boy?" Sure I didn't catch it at all and he says to my father, "That's why I have to take him for a months trial!"

I survived the first month anyway and Barry gave me the all clear and my father said to me, "Remember one thing now. Whatever is said to you, say nothing at all in return and that will get you through. No one wants to hear any young fellow giving him back-answers or cheek". So I was there two and a half years and I had terrible abuse to put up with but I worked hard. Sheep went up in price one time and we were told not to trim any chops from now on. This lady came in one morning and I started off with "Good morning madam now what can I do for you?" "I want three nice fat chops please", she said to me and I went and cut three nice fat chops and put them up on the scale and said "Four shillings and six pence please madam". "Excuse me", she said "I want you to trim around a little bit of the fat." I knew Barry was watching me but I took them back anyway and made them up again as light as I could and they came to four shillings and four pence. She was happy with that and away she went. "Come here boy. Were you not told some thing this morning?" Barry says to me "I was sir", said I. "And why aren't you doing it?" said he. "I was trying to please the lady sir. The lady wasn't happy with her chops I had to trim them a little bit." Then he said, "You had right to explain to her that you couldn't do it". "Well", I said, "I could of course but I wanted to hold her custom here and if she walked out and left them to me, you would say something else about it sir. I don't ever see you putting on your white coat and trying to please them." But I had made a mistake, and I knew it. "Get you coat boy", says Barry "and go away home". So I went and got my coat and went away to my digs.

Later that evening, the manager of the shop, John McNamara, arrived and asked me to come back. I said that, that morning was the time to do it and that they had let me off like a stray dog. There was a bit of a tattera at home then when I didn't want to go in anymore but my father went in and Barry told him that I was very attentive and very nice to the customers, but the most stubborn boy that ever worked for him. My father came back and told me this and that I would be taken back on the condition that I would apologise. "I won't apologise whatever will happen", I said. "You will have to do it for me", he said. "I won't", I said and I was twenty-one years of age at that time. So to make a long story short, it kind of upset my mother as well and she said to me "James, will you do it for me?" "I will Mam", I said. It broke my heart to apologise to that man because he did not deserve it as he was a tyrant. So that was the start of my life and my first job.

When I finished there, I was one of the few around who had papers for his trade. I got a job in town and a little place came up in Foynes about six or eight months after and my father bought it for me. I was up against heavy local opposition, people who were millionaires and could give meat away for nothing but I had a family so I had to pack up and sold out.

A lot of my friends went to England but they stayed around for a while until the dancing started, when we were sixteen, and every little dance we used go to was like a party as we all knew each other and had great fun. Next thing they went to England after the War and I think that was one of the great things that happened in this country. They had to work hard for farmers for twelve pound a month and thanks be to God, after the War, they got going in England. The whole place was blown down and it was up to them to build it up again. A lot of them are living there still but at the start, they were coming home delighted as it was the first break they ever got.

At that time, the butchers would get a fortnight's holiday but the apprentice would only get a week, and at that you wouldn't get a full week as you would have to be in for Saturday, the busy day. But the butcher's life then and a butcher's life today is very different and it has got very easy for them now. The electric saw was a blessing from God and has butchering made very, very easy. They have better ideas with regards bringing in the beast to kill and are more humane now, thank God. It's a great thing, you know, as it's bad for the meat to excite the animal. They get nervous and their blood pressure goes up and they don't bleed as well.

When I was young, we used to go hunting of a Sunday with a few old dogs and terriers and we loved that. We played football and loved that too and they were the only things we had as there was no television nor wireless when we were garsoons. I was on a football team at school and I remember we played our matches barefoot. There were clogs around all right with timber soles but they weren't much good for kicking.

During the War, when the tea and flour were rationed, it was hard enough to get by. Sometimes you would have to eat spuds twice a day and have tea only once. When my father would be saving the hay at home during that time, you would get black-market tea for a pound a pound (£/lb.) and he used to go mad over it and said it was the height of bla'guarding. But what could you do when you have to have it for the men in the meadow?

I went to Limerick at seventeen years of age in 1950, after the war. The city has doubled in size since and traffic was so slack then that you could drive cattle and sheep through it. Imagine if you tried to do that now! The city has advantages and disadvantages; you would hate to be in there in the summer time but it's grand to be there in the wintertime. It was then that I used to do a lot of dancing and would dance nearly three nights a week. There was Saint Michael's, Saint John's, Saint Munchin's, the Catholic Institute, and the Stella - five or six dance halls there all within walking distance. During Lent there was no dancing but there was a skating ring in one of the halls and they were awful dangerous but thank God, no one got seriously hurt.

The cinema in Limerick was an awful place for fleas you would have to tie the legs of your trousers when going in! But they did have very good films and I remember the huge queues for the film "The Quiet Man" when it opened.

I got an accordion when I was young and I learned away myself. I still play it and I love music, set dancing and the old time dancing. They call it ball-room dancing and adult dancing and it kind of frightens people away. It's lovely to have it because it keeps you young. An old lad like me, and my wife dead, wouldn't go to a disco no matter what. I would go to the adult dancing and it's lovely because we were used to it when we were young.

There was a great character up the road from us, Dinny Moroney, and he was friendly with Tom Cribbin, the publican. Dinny was fond of a few drinks but Tom never let him drink outside in the shop and would always let him into the kitchen. He would bring a lot of them in like that as it was very sociable and he was very nice and understood everybody. There was no such thing in Cribbin's pub as a two pence looking down on a penny, everybody was nice and would have the chat. But Dinny had a big family of nine and was a great man to work hard with horses on the road and would be drawing stones to the pier in Foynes with three horses. He used to carry his family to Mass and his wife would want him to bring a tankard of spring water in the trap on the way home. But he wouldn't, so he would bring them home from Mass first, put the tankard into the trap and down to the well with him but he would call into Cribbin's for a few pints and come home with the water then for the dinner. Then the stories would begin.

Dinny started, "I used to be carrying pigs to Limerick years ago for a half crown a pig and I had to wash out the car when I had the pigs delivered and I had a big canvas to put on the bottom of the car so I could bring home flour and meal. I went to bed early this night before I went to Limerick but before I did, I washed an apron for my mother, one of those that you would wrap it around you two or three times before you tie it, and I hung it out on the line. But by God, when I was going out later at quarter to two in the morning, the apron was gone. I went away anyway and I got in the next morning at around ten and my mother asked me if I had hung out her apron. "I did", I said, "but to tell you the truth it was gone when I was going out." We were both puzzled as to where it went. The next thing was, the old dog trotted around the corner and my mother said to me that that dog is going to have pups. "HE couldn't have pups", I said, "because that's a male dog." Then she said that there were two little paws coming out behind. So I went into the car house anyway and I got two bits of a rope, caught the old dog and I told my mother to hold him while I tied one bit of rope onto the neck of the dog and the other onto what was coming out behind. I tied that cord on to the gate and I carried him walking for about a mile but was nearly gone up past the Five Crosses before the last of the apron came out!"

He was inside with my father another day and when my father had the jobs done the two of then came in they were having a cup of tea and a bit of cold bacon with the bread and butter for the in the morning. My father threw down a bit of a skin from the bacon on the floor and the little cat that was there ran out and picked it up. My father told Dinny that the cat had only one eye but still she was a great one and he had often seen her making one hop outside and catching a mouse. "By God", says Dinny "cats are very clever. I was above on the old donkey and trap one time, and the Missus was going to Shanagolden. She had young turkeys in the yard and she asked me to sit down there and mind them until she came back and I said I would. While I was sitting down smoking my pipe, there was little cat, smaller than your one but she would have very big kittens, and I saw her and another one and I knew well that they were talking. I watched them anyway and didn't the mother go up across the road into your meadow and whatever look down I gave, didn't I spot a rabbit a good bit out from the ditch. Next thing, she came out from your place, over the ditch and stole up and caught and killed the rabbit. She was trying to drag it up through the grass but it was a bit high and honest to God, didn't she come up for the kittens to go down and give her a hand!" Oh, Old Dinny, he was an awful case and he had terrible good yarns but was a great man and looked after his family well.

Christmas was great in those days but the major difference is that it is all turkeys today. Then, you would get a great goose for a pound and so more people ate them. Santa used come to everyone, believe it or not, but he wouldn't be overloaded, though you would always get something. I used to get little horses, cows, little motor cars and little handy little things like that which made us very happy. Old lads like myself would say that the youngsters are not enjoying themselves like we did. They are they are having a great time because they have more money and they are just as happy as we were, but it's very sad and sickening to hear boys and girls taking drugs, it's a pity and a shame for them.

On Stephen's Day, you had the Wren and it is still going great today in places and I would still go on it myself. We go out for charity now and for the senior citizens. They have a great day out and their Christmas dinners come down from Newcastle and they would have music and they dance around and it's lovely. The senior citizens get a good run these days and I am delighted for them. It's a funny thing but often I play a bit of music for them on the buses here and there and whatever it is, older people are sometimes a bit critical of young people but you know, when they take a few jars themselves, they are just as bad as them!

In my opinion, it was easier to raise a family in olden days. Our family experienced the War years when you would have cocoa or tea for your evening meal and very little flour to make anything. People started to grow wheat and get it crushed and made "one-way" bread, as they called it. It wasn't as nice as the ordinary cake of bread and it was very brown, but you had nothing else. Today, the majority of people have fresh meat every day but the only day that we had fresh meat was on a Sunday. It was bacon every other day and there was no such thing as rashers and sausages. If you felt hungry for your tea, off you go and get a couple of cuts of home cure bacon and bread and that was the way it was.

I met my wife in Foynes at a Ceili in 1956 and we were married two years later. We married young and that time there were no mortgages around and the man working would have to be able to support the family on his own. It is very hard on youngsters today and often they have to have two jobs to keep going. I had my own business at the time but the wages were about seven or eight pound a week and people were flying it on that. Factory workers in Foynes were earning five and six pounds a week and they might get a bit of over time to get it up to seven pounds. So life was easier than now, I think.

I am retired now for the last couple of years and I got used to being so. I thought I would never cope at the start but I keep canaries and I look after those. Then, I have to cook for my own lads at home and that passes the day for me again. I still am playing a bit of music and I enjoy that. To sum up my life, I am going on for sixty-nine years of age and to be honest with you, it's been like one big long day. That's as sure as God is! It travelled so fast and it is so short that it will amaze you. You have to do your best, look after your family and hope for the rest then. We will all meet in Heaven hopefully and if there is no Heaven there, won't we all get a terrible hop! I hope that it is there and I believe that it is there.

1933: One of the greatest classic films of all time, King Kong, is released.

The first transatlantic jet passenger service, started by BOAC, takes place between New York and London, ***October 4th 1958***.

Abbeyfeale School Group of 1939

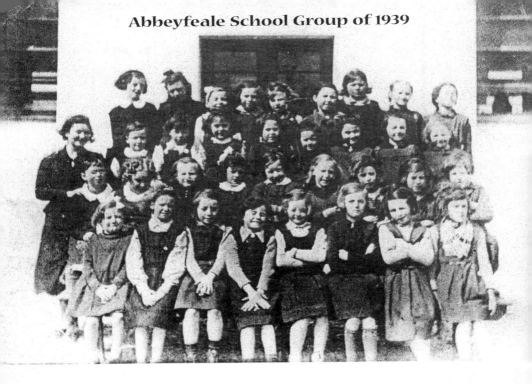

Corpus Christi procession, Abbeyfeale, c.1900

Askeaton Abbey

Main Street, Ballyhahill

Charlie Fealey's pony and trap with Betty and Lisa Reidy

Curragh Chase, Kilcornan

Coopering Tools

Fennessey's Bar, Barrigone, Foynes

Post Office, Feoghanagh

Foynes Station House

Fullers Folly and Arra River, Newcastle West

Begley's Forge, Bridge St., Abbeyfeale

BEGLEY

Beagh Castle, Ballysteen

Begley's Forge - Bellows

Grotto, Cahermoyle

Hamilton Tower, Glin

Lime Kiln

Killeedy Castle

Hobnail Boots and Last

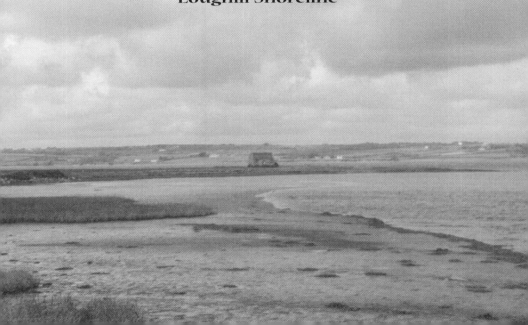

Loughill Shoreline

Halla Inse Bán, Templeglantine

Old Cottage, Foynes Island

Michael Nolan piking turf

Forge Wheel, Castlemahon

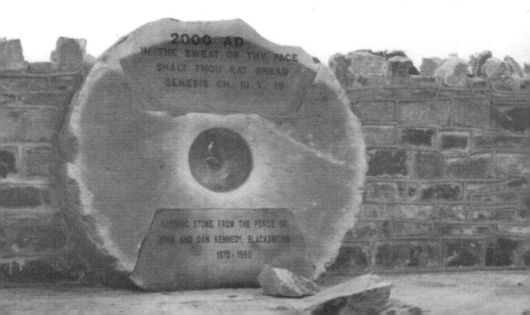

Old Mill, Newbridge, Creeves

Protestant graveyard, Ardgoul-South, Cappagh

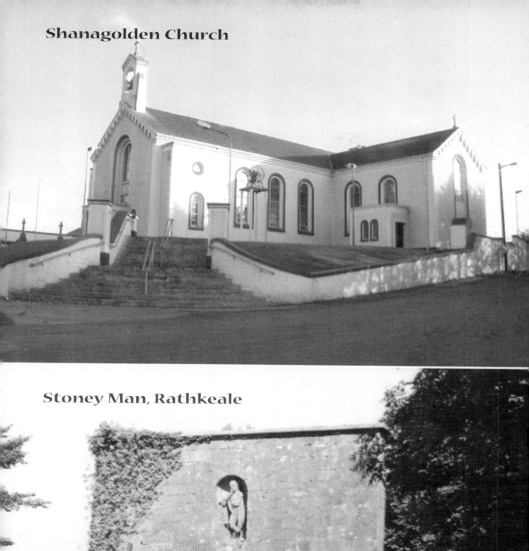

Shanagolden Church

Stoney Man, Rathkeale

St. Bernard's Well, Rathkeale

St. James' Well, Ardagh

St. Kieran's Well,
Clonagh, Coolcappa

Old Shop front,
Ballingarry

Village Pump, Feenagh

Thatched Cottage, Newcastle West

Turf cutters at work

Turf footed along the bank

Lisnacullia Castle

Fr. Casey's Statue, Abbeyfeale

Memorial, Broadford

Shanagolden Market, c. 1950's

Miss Woulfe, teacher in Abbeyfeale, photograph taken in 1957

Michael O'Donnell with his father, Bill O'Donnell

James Flynn

James Flynn is my name of Pallas, Kilmeedy, Co. Limerick. I was born on the 25th of February 1927 on a farm in Feohanagh belonging to my grandfather. I remember my father was five foot nine inches tall but could jump over six feet, and he came from Belleville. My mother came from Kerry and was training with the nuns while there. There were twelve of us in our family, but there were six cot deaths, so there are only six of us left at present. After seven years and some few months, we left my grandfathers' place in Feoghanagh and it was sold by public auction, but later, my father would drink all the money we got for it. This place here in Kilmeedy was belonging to my grandfather also, and he left it to me before he died in 1935. He also left us money to help us survive, as times were tough.

When I was going to school in Feohanagh, Mrs. Crystal and Master Kelly were teaching me. Mrs. Crystal was very hard and if you were late coming into school, you would get a beating. I often got one as I had to go the long way to school, because if you came by Young's short-cut you might meet a bull and would have to take the long way around anyway. In the school in Kilmeedy, Master Reidy was teaching me and he also gave me a lot of beatings.

Before I left school, I would go out during my holidays working on a farm for one of the neighbours. I would be below until all hours of the night and he had me worked to death for six pence a day, or ten shillings a week, and that was my pay. Often I worked six days a week and sometimes seven.

I started to train in 1930, when I was three years old. I could stand on my hands, walk on my hands, stand on my head without hands, balance myself with one hand, and do a cartwheel with one hand. That was my first training in the field here in Kilmeedy. Later, I was quite good at the 100 yards and the other short courses. I had the full gear with spiked shoes and everything and I was fairly lively. My style was that I would trail in the final, then, coming up the straight, I could strike out, move direct and straight and no interfering with anyone. If I didn't win, I would shake hands with the man in front of me.

I went to every type of sport on my bicycle. I went to a hurling match there one time, the time Mick Mackey was playing against Christie Ring. I have seen Paddy Clohessy playing, he was a great full-back man and a great man for Limerick. I also saw Paddy Scanlon below in Adare and he was an outstanding hurler. I traveled all over to see Cloncagh-Knockaderry or Feohanagh-Castlemahon play.

At the age of sixteen, I went into the Army and thought it was outstanding. It was during World War Two and that time the Germans were inclined to invade. I served twenty years in the army but there was this one captain who was a very cruel man. He never got an inch in me because I went never out of line or broke anything and all of the other boys would come in and they'd wreck the place.

There were three pubs in Feohanagh that people went to; Murphy's, Cussens and Flanagan's, around 1933, and I would have been six years old that time. You had the pictures and the dances on the side of the road, and Davie Roche and Jimmy Mc Carthy playing the fiddle up in the house and they were gifted musicians.

There are fairy forts all over this land but I remember Jim Moore, the man who lived to be a hundred years old, tried divining a nearby fort for gold but with no success. I would never go into them as you are not to interfere with them. I was with Tim Curtain, the famous water diviner, for a while going around finding water. One day, we were in a field looking for a spring but he couldn't find anything so he laid his hands out on me and transferred his powers to me. He then asked me to test the water to see what depth it was. I got the sally rod and the watcher (a weight on a string) and walked through the field a bit. I turned around and told him that at a depth of thirty-five feet, there was a double spring. But, I found out after, he was only testing me. Then another day, in another field, I got four springs and I said nothing about them and Timmy came on to find them but he was on the ball with them. I was trying to test him!

If your wedding ring is lost, let it be gold, silver, or copper, I'll know it. I can read the cards there for anyone, but I wouldn't play them, I'd only read them. I can tell a pregnant woman by swaying my watch across her stomach if she was going to have a boy or a girl. I could tell if a person is coming to rob me, but I wouldn't be able to see them. I would know it but I couldn't say anything. Anything that was taken out of this house I would know who it was that did it, even if I were miles away from them. It isn't through the Devil that I am working at all, he never gave me any of those things, but you must have a bit of faith and a bit of religion for these things to work.

---

*It was announced in **December 1927** that over £16,000 had been donated for the relief of the dependants of the Dromcollogher fire.*

Jeremiah Foley

My name is Jeremiah Foley of 3 St. Ita's Road, Abbeyfeale but I was born on Abbeyfeale Hill. There was fifteen of us in my family, well, there is one dead now, so there is fourteen of us left, but there was twenty-one of us altogether, between dead and alive. My mother lived to be ninety-four.

We didn't take any notice of there being fifteen in the house, we were happy out. But we had nothing that time. Christ, there was nothing. Today, I have three sisters and two brothers in England and the rest of them are living locally, but back then, with a big family, the half sack of flour wouldn't last too long.

There was no range at that time, only the open fire, but there was this oven with a cover on it. The oven had three legs and a cover on it and as well as the fire underneath you'd have to have a good red fire up on top of the cover when you were baking.

My father was a labourer and he worked for the County Council. They found it hard to raise a family that time. You'd get a half sack of flour for a pound and they used to do all their own baking from that, and also they'd kill a pig every year. There was a lot of children there that time but most people had a big family.

We'd walk to school in Dromtrasna, which wasn't far from us up on the hill above. The thing was, we were barefoot that time and they used to put broken stones in potholes on the road to fix them and they would cut the toes off you. There would be many children walking to school together that time. Overall, I liked it and thought the teachers were okay. I didn't go to school a lot of the time because, when I was only twelve years of age, I was sort of working and going to school at the same time as I was the eldest in the family.

I was out in service then at fourteen years of age and went working for farmers. I gave two years at Jimmy Jamesy's in Kilconlea, and he had a pig farm. A fellow of fourteen isn't able to do a lot but you'd job around all right. I'd be jobbing around and minding the young lad, the child that was born when I was there, and is now the man that's there today, Jamesy. I used be minding him because his mother used to go to town every Monday. I was getting ten pounds for the year and the employers were good.

I also worked for Con Rourke in Clash, who they used to call the "Miracle Rourke". Later, I worked for Mick Lyons above in Dromtrasna. It was all farming, and the biggest wage I ever got was fifty pounds for the year. That wasn't a bad wage for anyone at that time.

Time off was scarce and you would do the same thing every day, even on Holy days. You'd go to Mass and things like that, but back to work after. There was no such thing as holidays. You were working from the 1st of February to Christmas and that was your year, eleven months or so.

Almost anybody in a job would be working with farmers that time. The labourers would come to the hiring fair in Abbeyfeale and someone would hire them for the year. Then, it was all according to the bargain you would make with them, but they mightn't give you what you'd be looking for in the end though.

It was all farmers I worked for up to 1963. I then worked with a contractor, Nicholas Cotter, to whom I gave ten or twelve years. He used to do work for the P&T (Post & Telegraph) and also did sewers and other kinds of contract work. There was better wages with him.

I remember one time I was working in Knocklong, down in the sewers. There was ten or twelve of us working on the job from all different places. We were inside in a trench across from the railway and there was a twenty-foot cast iron pipe to be put in beneath the railway, all the rest were concrete pipes. There was a man at one end and I was at the other end and he told me to hand him up the pick-axe, but whatever happened, the pick-axe was whipped out of my hand and I was caught as far as the waist inside in the trench. Whatever about me, your man at the other end was killed stone dead when the trench fell in. If I had waited for a split second, I was gone. The work was dangerous all right, you see, and the trench should have been shored up with timber because, with the trains passing, there were vibrations which knocked it in.

I went to a match in Dublin once in 1946 and I wasn't there since. It was Kerry and Roscommon that played in it. It was a good game, although Kerry were beaten in the last two minutes and they were out.

We used to keep a few greyhounds before and I remember I sold two greyhounds to a neighbour, Pat Collins, and I bought another hound over in 'Glantine with the money I got from the sale. He was a great greyhound and won many coursing races. He was favourite to win the St. Leger at the track in Limerick and I was getting five hundred pounds for him inside in the box before the race. I couldn't part with him, I wouldn't sell him. As it turned out, he was killed in the race. I don't know what happened, but it seems he broke his neck or something at the third bend. 'Just Faun' was his name.

There was the hall that time for entertainment and you'd be going out on Sunday night to the dance up there in Tom Tobin's. It was six pence to get in, I think and it was less than that before but it rose to six pence. They were complaining about it as it was too dear. Well, that's going back a long time now.

I used to play cards myself. I love them but I haven't played now for years. Some of the houses around would raffle something during the game. There was no bit of music or dance or anything, it was just the game of cards.

I can't place the first television but I remember the first radio all right. We used to travel a couple of miles to where there would be one to hear the football matches. Radios were scarce that time and there would be a big crowd coming to the house where there was one.

I was walking for years but at the same time, there were lots of us walking. I remember a car up at Con Leahy's, Sean Leahy's father, and that was the first around here in this part of the country anyway. It was a Baby Ford and they were a small car.

Christmas was good all right, but there weren't any decorations that time. Yerrah, we had nothing, there was no such thing as toys then or even a good bit after. The place is full of them and it is too many of them they have now and they have no mass whatever in them. There would be turkeys all right, and my father used keep them at that time and he used bring them into Abbeyfeale to sell them.

There is a holy well in Dromtrasna, above in Kilineach, and I was up there several times. One of the priests here in Abbeyfeale would go up and say mass on the pattern day. When I was working with Mick Lyons up in Dromtrasna, the well was only a small bit away from me, in Cotter's place.

I am living thirty-four years at my present address. I lived in Mountmahon for twelve years, over beside the factories, before I got the house. I'll tell you now where I met my partner. There was a raffle above in Roger Finnerty's, an old thatched house that time, and there was coursing on in Newcastle and I went to the coursing that day cycling and it poured rain. When I was coming home, I went to the raffle to dry off and it was there I met her.

The three girls are married; one is married in Lyrecrompane, and there's one married in Glin and there's another married in Templeglantine. I have one son, John, but I don't know will he marry at all, but we're lucky to have him now because we're getting old.

New Years Day 1958 brings the news that Sean South was shot and killed in a raid on an army barracks in Co. Fermanagh.

Air India jet crashes off the Irish coast in **June 1985**, *with the loss of 329 lives.*

Jim Ronan

Jim Ronan is my name and I live in Boherbui, Newcastle West now. I was born in East Strand, Monagea, three miles outside the town of Newcastle West. My father was a farmer on a small company farm.

I went to Monagea National School with Tony Hough and after that I went to the Tech. where I did the Group Cert. in 1951. At school, I played handball and had a great interest in all sport and in all matches. I had an Irish teacher from Kerry, Sean Sullivan was his name, who used to teach us Irish songs.

After the Group Cert I went to Dublin for six months, learning bar work. I worked in a place called Stepaside until 1952 but the money was small so I came home. I did some farming here, but later I joined Telecom Éireann, who I spent twenty-five years with as a technician. The wages when I started in Telecom were £2.50 a week, much like what you'd get in Dublin.

Religion in the nineteen forties and fifties was a major thing and you had to go to mass and confession. I see changes compared to then and there is more freedom now. The priest used to come to the school every week, Canon Lyons from Ballingarry, and he was the inspector that time.

I remember Christmas when it was real Christmas. There were no toys nor fancy goods, only the simple things like stockings. I used to walk to midnight mass in Monagea and there would be a big crowd going then. Christmas day was great, with all the family together, the goose for dinner and a big turf fire with logs. We'd light candles in every window and decorate them with holly and ivy.

In that time, people would never marry during Lent and they waited until after Easter to do so. Lent was strict in those days. In my mother and father's time, on Ash Wednesday and Good Friday, they used to drink the tea black and we had no meat and only one meal. The people used to give up their pints and cigarettes for Lent and then they'd hand up the money. I used to have great sport at Easter, boiling as many eggs as I could find, duck eggs or goose eggs, whatever the case may be.

We went to the holy well in Monagea on the fifteenth of August, and in the fifties, it would be packed with people, with the priest saying the rosary and the people going around the well three times saying the rosary also. I still visit St. Bridget's Well in Newcastle on the first of February.

I like travelling, Irish music, song, dancing and the craic at Lisdoonvarna. Anything Irish, I like. I dance Irish polka sets and I am full time dancer. Nash's Cinema was the main one here in Newcastle West when I was young and there was a dance hall there as well. I used to go dancing in Tournafulla, the Old Mill Hall, Listowel Hall and the Devon Road, Abbeyfeale. All the dances were cheap that time, three shillings and six pence would get you in, and I used to travel by bicycle, as there were not many cars that time. I went to crossroad dances and to the jigs and rallies in Monagea. The rallies were a great thing because there would be porter and wine, with lemonade for the girls. We would join the Wren crowd where we would be telling stories, dancing polkas and old-time waltzing. There would often be fifty of us in a batch, with a tambourine and accordion, and we would get twenty pounds between us.

In farming in my day, the milking was done by hand. I'd cut hay with a scythe and pike it after, cut and pike turf in my own time, like my father, who did a lot of work long ago. I did all kinds of work. I mixed cement and laid a few blocks and I did a lot of manual labour when I first started at Telecom, like digging holes, three a day at four feet deep. I finished up as a foreman at Telecom, having started from scratch. They used to send materials from Dublin in the carriages to the old train station in Newcastle and I knew all the men working there, like John Whelan, Minnie Donovan, and Denis O'Grady. Liam Madigan was a great fellow and he knew all about the train station. The last train to go through Barnagh and on to Kerry was in 1975, twenty-six years ago. The Great Southern Trail Project has started since then.

My work with Telecom took me all over Ireland - to Dublin, Longford, Ennis, Charleville and Listowel. You would notice things too, like in Longford, there would be different customs to here and their talk would be different. Kerry and Limerick had much the same accent. They had their own slang in different counties too. For example, in Kildare they would say " *it's a hardy one*", and in Cork they might have "*Are you right there boy?*" and so on. Our language is very straight altogether in West Limerick and North Kerry.

I remember when I was working here in Newcastle West, there was only two houses on both sides of the road from Monagea to Newcastle West. Now there are sixty or seventy on the way, the best of new houses. The electricity came in the late fifties and we had no telephone or electricity at home until then, only lamps with paraffin oil. We had no washing machine either, only an old scrubber and we used to wash ourselves in a tub. There was no bathroom or anything.

There was no transport, only the bicycle, and I walked a lot. There were very few cars going to the creamery but you had the horse and donkey and car. The first motor car around here, I'd say, was belonging to Tom O'Connell in Knockane or Murtie Shine in Boherbui. They both were driving around the same time. Murtie told me that he was driving for sixty-four years and he never had an accident in his life.

The television came in 1964 and the first match I saw was Limerick playing Roscommon. I remember the crowd going into Jack Mullanes pub in Strand, as he was the first public house to have a television and it was the real thing. And it was Micheál Ó Heir who brought the matches completely into the houses. I am writing a poem about him at the moment. I remember in the nineteen forties he was broadcasting matches on the radio from Thurles and Croke Park and all that. It was like a great gathering in the houses, the excitement of it all.

I remember some of the major happenings in Newcastle West, like the burning of the hotel in Maiden Street, where Ned Kenny's is now, in sixty or sixty-one, and the time Nash's Cinema was burned down on the North Quay. The fairs were a big thing for the people around, and especially for the farmers, who used to grow their own vegetables and sell them there but small farmers are scaled out now and their machinery are antiques.

At the Abbeyfeale calf market my father used to sell calves at five or six pounds apiece that time. He would leave at six o'clock in the morning to meet the buyers from town going to where the market was on, and there was often terrible battling going on over the price of a calf. There were pig fairs in Newcastle and the horse fairs in Listowel and Knocknagree, and I used to go just to see the fun and for a day out.

I had only one brother and he died of cancer in 1962. He was a young man of only twenty-six. My father's people went to America and I have first cousins in Chicago. My mother was an only daughter so I have no relations in this country. My father was a great character and he used to tell a lot of yarns. He was involved in politics and he was elected to Dail Éireann as a full time Fianna Fail deputy. I am not involved in politics but I know it has changed very much since my father's time from what I read about it in the papers and books.

I used to play cards in my younger days and played a bit of poker, but preferred '45' or '41'. I have great interest in sport, hurling and football, and since the fifties, have gone to most All Ireland hurling and football matches. I have seen Kerry in the seventies and Tipperary in the eighties. I have seen a lot of the great players like Jimmy Doyle, Liam De Vally, Mick O'Connell, Mickey Sheehy and Bomber Liston, Eamon Creagan, and John Doyle of Tipperary. I have great interest in those great players.

I think technology changed people completely. The young know more today than I did at fifteen going to school. We were more innocent in bygone days but we were brought up kind of backward really. I was very close to my father and mother, and I used to stay at home more at night. There would be a gathering of seanchaí and great card games, stories of fairies and of bygone days that seem to have all gone now. The people were friendlier and you could leave your door open and needn't lock it. I feel the richness of the 'Celtic Tiger' is a great thing, but the old people came out much better off as they were friendly and more neighbourly. There was no murder, rape or anything - it just wasn't heard of in my time.

Since I have retired from Telecom, I've read many history and sports books. I go to the library every second evening, where I read all the papers and I get an average of two to three books a week. I think the library is a great place for children with all types of book there for them. I am in a lot of organisations here in Newcastle West, such as the Old IRA Monument group, the Famine Graveyard group and the Great Southern Trail Walk, and I would walk three or four miles a day myself.

These are some words my mother used to say to me -
Turn backwards, turn backwards, how time is in flight.
Just make me a child again for a night.

---

*In **April 1951**, National census shows that the population of the Republic of Ireland is 2,960,593, and that the population in Northern Ireland is 1,370,921.*

***1963:** Ireland applies for, and is turned down for, membership of the European Economic Commission.*

Josephine Goggin

My name is Josephine Goggin of Coolbeg, Kildimo, Co. Limerick and I was born in 1914. There was one boy and three girls and myself in my family. I had a sister in the convent in Kilfinnane and I had a sister in Philadelphia and both of them died within one year of each other. My mother is dead for years as well. She was seventy-five and my father was eighty-four when he died.

I went to school to my two aunts, Mrs Cahill and Kitty Goggin. And no, it wasn't easier for me at all. I got the same treatment as the rest. They weren't very different teachers from nowadays but we got slapped and that is very different from now. I was never sent to secondary school but my two sisters went to Limerick and I stayed at home when I was sixteen years.

I never got a job as I worked at home on the farm. It was hard enough but it would have been easier now if they had milking machines and everything like they do today. We had to do it all with our hands; wash the tanks, wash the buckets and send the milk off to the creamery. We had a big garden of potatoes, turnips and mangles and they also had to be picked by hand. The corn and hay and all that had to be done too, you know what a farm is like.

I remember the threshing well. We had a lot of corn at that time and Madigans down the road had a threshing machine and it was they that did all our threshing for us. There would always be a crowd, maybe fourteen or fifteen, in for the threshing. Oh Lord, I don't know how it was done, but they'd put in the corn and wheat into one end of the machine and it would come out of different sections of it. I suppose it would take a good few hours to get it done.

I would get up always at seven o'clock during the cutting of the hay. The cutting of the hay is different now. It was with a machine that we used to cut the hay with at that time. Nowadays, with the silage, it is very different. There are no windes of hay now. You'd make windes and you'd draw them home and into the haggard and you'd make a big long reek of it. We had a donkey and cart and we had a horse and a dray car and a float for bringing the hay.

It was a small farm. We used to keep pigs, milk cows and feed calves. We had no one working for us ever as my father used to do all the work. He was a great worker. I had a few turkeys myself, only two or three, that you'd have for Christmas. We had plenty of old hens and ducks and we sold eggs but we used a lot of them. We always took animals to the fair and my father, he always walked up to the fair at Rathkeale and God, after walking it up, you might have to bring home the cattle again as there would be no sale for them.

There was great entertainment in the past. The neighbours used to come in to play a game of cards in the houses in the wintertime. Then there was a dance hall not too far away and there would be a dance there maybe once a week. Oh Lord, it would be very little to go into the dance hall at that time. I think about a half a crown. At home we had gramophones, they came out first, and then we had the wireless and then television after that. We never had any light until they came around with the electricity and we had no running water in either until they came around to put it in. There wasn't much of a change when the televisions came in as many people would be in and out of the house the whole time. Well, the older people would come in anyway.

I always remember a drama show going around. I don't know the name of them now but we had them in the parish for three weeks. God, they were great and they did all the plays. An awful lot came down from Ballingarry and other places. Fr. Lyons, the old man, he used to bring down the dramatic classes. I always thought that I was very good at them. There was also a travelling cinema run by the Gazettes and God, we used to go to them and it was only a shilling to get in. I remember them well. There wasn't many nice films around and anyway it wasn't always the best, as there used often be breakdowns in them.

At school, we had always to say the Angelus and we had always to say a prayer at the starting of our day. There was two catechisms, the red one and the green one, and, oh the Lord save us and guard us, for the Confirmation we had special classes and it was very hard. We had bible history and you had to learn it off by heart before we got our Confirmation and we used to have classes on Sundays after Mass. It is so easy now that they are asked very little. Oh, the Bishop, he would ask plenty questions and every one of us were asked a couple of questions on the day. We never went anywhere the day of the Confirmation. Oh no, we were never taken anywhere. We just had a meal at home. Now, they are taken out to hotels and places. It is a different life altogether. I kept on all my life the same as usual. I kept on saying my prayers and saying the rosary. My favourite saint is Padre Pio.

The Holy Well was about four miles away from me in Kilbreedy, near Stonehall, and there was said to be cures from it. There was a man who lost his eyesight and his wife took him around the well and he got it back. There was three or four more cures there. The water used to be lovely there. At home now, we had a well down the field and there used to be lovely water in it. We didn't have to dig the well as, somehow or another, it was there for as long as I could remember.

It was always a goose we had for Christmas, and it used to be a very good time. We had always the candles lighting and we'd be looking out for gifts and what we'd get in our stockings. Not very much though! We always had three masses on Christmas Day. St. Patrick's day was also great and we always had our shamrocks on and we used to go to the parades, not very much where I lived, but more in the cities.

I remember the wakes in the houses long ago and everyone in the area used to turn up and everyone would be dressed in black. When my mother died, all the neighbours called in and there would be always be a drop of drink or a cup of tea for them. At that time, everybody was waked at home but now they are taken to the morgues. The corpse at the wake wouldn't be in a coffin. They would be dressed up in bed and I always remember it was an old lady that came in to dress my mother. You would have a habit at that time, a brown habit, and candles lighting and the curtains would be closed always. They would also cover the looking glass. I don't know what the reason was but isn't that funny how you'd cover a looking glass as well if you had thunder and lighting outside. It is kind of a tradition, I suppose.

The length of time for the wake would depend on when the person died. My mother died during the day and she was waked that night until the next day, when she was taken to the church at about six or seven o'clock. It was always the undertakers that removed them from the house and that time, horses and a carriage were always used.

I remember the time of the curfew, the time of the Black and Tans. You could have nobody in your home after ten o'clock at night. I remember the Tans coming as a child. I remember them coming to our house and searching the place to see if you had anyone hiding there. Down the road further, I remember they took away a man by the name of Hartnett. They had these terrible big tanks on wheels going down the road and you'd hear them coming from nearly half a mile away. When they'd be passing, my mother would take us out to the back yard for fear of any damage they'd do to the house or to us.

During the Second War and the time of the rations, you would get a book of coupons and you'd only get a half-ounce of tea, depending how many you had in the house, but Lord, it would never be enough. We had to use coffee and all with that and it still wouldn't do you only for two days and then, we were rationed in soap! Yeah, rationed in soap. We had coupons but the soap used to do us for a good while, you see. We had plenty of flour because my father used to take the wheat to get it ground and you'd have wheaten flour then and it used to make lovely bread.

There is an awful difference nowadays compared to when I was young. The youngsters, they love going to school, they like being educated, and they like to travel, which we didn't like to do at all. I was in America three times, for my sister was there at that time. I stayed for nine months each time and it was great. I'd say now the last trip I made was twenty-five years ago. I went over all by myself that time.

My brother inherited the farm but he is not there now. He is in my house now because he lost the sight in one of his eyes. Because my house is near the village, he has home help from a girl there.

I'm here in the Tall Trees Nursing Home in Askeaton for the past three years and I like it very much. Sure, it's like being at home, you have great company and you can talk to everybody.

---

*First World War breaks out, **August 4th 1914**.*

*Elvis the King Presley dies on the **16th August 1977**.*

Joseph Downes

I'm Joe Downes of Bishop Street, Newcastle West. I was born in Pallaskenry in October 1935 and I lived there until I came to Newcastle West in 1965. I went to school in Pallaskenry, to the National School, and I then went to the Christian Brothers secondary school for two years. I worked with McCarthy's, the Woollen Merchants, in Limerick and then I joined the Air Corps when I was seventeen.

I worked in Limerick, I suppose, for a year after leaving school, when I was fifteen and then I was in the Air Corps. I was with Donnelly Sausages as a salesman from 1956 to 1962, and I finally came to live in Newcastle West in 1965. They were all very good jobs and everyone was very nice to me. I was three months in the Curragh but I was based in Balldonnell, I was supposed to be learning to be a mechanic but I got out on compassionate grounds.

It was wool I was working with in Limerick. Washing the sheep's wool when the sheep would be sheared and they had the big washing machine to wash it. Then I was six years with Donnelly's but I was living in Pallaskenry and I didn't come to Newcastle West until 1965. The Ballroom had already opened in 1960.

My father was a butcher and my mother had work enough at home. There was no women working that time when they were married. I had five sisters and three brothers and there was nine of us in the family. One of my sisters died in 1940 and another in '41. My mother died in '41 and my father died six years later.

I think in Pallaskenry at that time there was four pubs and maybe four or five shops. Now as far as I know there are only two pubs at the moment.

I opened the Olympic Ballroom in 1960. It always went well, so I left Donnellys and it was a full time job doing the ballroom. Usually, we had two nights a week, Fridays and Sundays. Sundays were the big night then. I had all the big bands; Joe Dolan, Brendan Bowyer, Dickie Rock, and we had Joe Locke and Annie McLoughlin, the Everly Brothers, Mudd, Phil Lynott and Sinead O'Connor. Those bands that time would be as big as U2 are now. I was my own boss that time. I think when we opened though, it was ten shillings to get in that time, which is now fifty pence, and after that they paid six old pence for minerals, which would be the same as two and a half pence now.

I think the Olympic closed in 1985 and I had the River Room then with Donnie Collins until we sold it in 1994. We opened it in 1968 and that took over from the Olympic, as there was no drink in the Olympic, and now, unfortunately, people will only go where there is drink.

Religion was big in my time and my brother, who went to America in 1961, was the parish clerk in Pallaskenry. Even when the ballroom opened there were hardly any girls dancing and there were an awful lot of pioneers that time. I'd say that after every dance, you'd find a lost pioneer pin.

I remember John Barrett, the publican of the Greyhound Bar, telling me when I took him to a funeral out in Ardagh, that he preferred one half an hour of a dance, and this was later on in the 1970's, than the whole of a market day in Newcastle West.

There were fairs that time too but I'd say they were nearly over by the time I came to Newcastle West. It was cattle fairs they had then. There are fierce changes in Newcastle West, it was only a small place in that time. I remember when Scanglo was built and Newcastle West has come a long way since.

I was one of the founder members of the soccer club in Pallaskenry, and at that time, you'd have Foynes and Askeaton, Mungret and Newcastle West as the only five or six teams playing soccer. Now, it is in every parish in Ireland.

The only thing, I suppose, with the entertainment that time was that there was no drink as such, there was no going to the bar except for a very odd night in the Olympic and people used to come at eight o'clock in the evening. Nowadays, if you haven't drink in the place, they won't come at all. At that time, all the dance halls used to have to close down for Lent, and a big night out was Shrove Tuesday night, the start of Lent. We didn't open then again until Easter Sunday night. Most of the bands at that time used to have to go to England during Lent.

---

*The Italian invasion of Abyssina (now Ethopia), which was being ruled by Emperor Haile Selassie, begins in **October 1935**, led by Mussolini.*

__1960__: In Britain, the Betting & Gambling Act was passed, which allowed betting shops, nightclubs, bingo halls and gambling casinos to operate.

Margaret Lynch

My name is Margaret Lynch of Kilbradran, Shanagolden, County Limerick but I was born in Morgans, Barrigone, in 1931. There were four of us in the family. Today, there is one in Kinigad, one in Dublin, one in Kilbaha, Askeaton, and I am here in Kilbradran.

The first thing I remember in life was the importance of religion. It was very important and you went to mass even if you had no way of going. You went if you were able to walk there, even through five fields and a mile of a road. You went to a mission, which lasted seven days a week, once every three years, and we walked three times a day to it at Robertstown Church from our place, which was seven miles away, when it was on.

I walked to school in Barrigone, through five fields and a half-mile of road. There were no buses back then and life going to school was very good and very different to now.

We worked after school and worked in the evenings. But it was all to the good. We all sat around the fire at night. There were no televisions; we played on combs, and my father told stories. It was very nice and it was a different life to now altogether.

My father was a farmer and we helped out on the farm every Saturday. We were out pulling weeds off the corn; we weeded the turnips and other different things. My father, with the machinery and horses, did the heavy work and we did the weeding, the small work. I worked at home all the time but then I went to an invalid aunt and spent two or three years with her working for nothing.

There was no electricity at that time either. My sister Maureen used a lamp to read as she sat by the fire at night. I always remember that after the schoolwork was done she would read to us. She was a terror for reading and she read all of the different stories out of that book that was going at the time, "Our Boys". She also brought home library books and we sat around listening to stories, often until twelve o'clock at night, with the light of the fire and of the lamp keeping us company.

We used all walk back to Barrigone Well for the Pattern Day. We would be looking forward to it for ages, what with all the races and the sweets that would be there. You'd see the ass carts with the heel of it down in the ground and it propped up with something and it always filled with sweets and ice-cream and different things. Then there were the sports in the field beside the well. We were young that time and we did not understand about the praying part of it, but if we did not get there, we would lose our heads! You would pray your request around the well by saying so many decades of the Rosary. They came from everywhere to that well and there were people cured there, they say.

It was always a marvellous day and it is still there, of course, but there are no sports or sweets for sale now. Of course, the pub was at the evening's finish and the old fellows would be outside playing melodeons. It was Corbett's at that time but it is Hennessey's pub now.

In August and September, we had the forty shades of green in the fields, and in the gardens, there were turnips, mangles, potatoes, everything in all different colours. It was beautiful to look at them all.

You'd kill a pig once a year and put him in the barrel. There were big dinners in every house you went into because you had your own fresh vegetables, you had your own potatoes, and we had our own flour from the corn.

Christmas Eve would come and my mother would be stuffing the turkey. They were real Christmases that time. Today, it is not too bad, compared to England, where they have very dull Christmases. I found an awful change when I was there last year. You had the Mass all right, but there was no fuss, because they all do their shopping in October! Not the same as here at all.

The preparation for Christmas is different too. I remember they used to white wash the houses, all the boarded floors would be scrubbed and the holly was put over the pictures and everywhere.

I well remember the night before I got my Confirmation. We would buy big lorries of turf that would come once a year and we were expecting a load that night. But the turf did not come and I was sent out for sticks for the fire, a job I loved to do. They said at home that I was like Bernadette in Lourdes. I went down across the fields and I brought about four barths of sticks on my back. On my way out, a big pile of bullocks came after me and frightened the life out of me. Now I was only twelve at this stage and all my mother was worried about was that she was waiting to wash my hair for the Confirmation the next day!

The next day, we all went off in the pony and trap. My uncle came for the one that was getting their Confirmation because he had a big pony and trap and we had only a smaller one, and he took us back to Robertstown. You got your Confirmation, you came home, and you might have an extra biscuit for tea. There was no big days out, no big lay out, out you went and played around the field. No photographs, no nothing.

My sisters were raging as they wanted to go back to Aughinish to take photos. They had a camera between the two of them but they would not be allowed back or be allowed ramble away like that. So we have no photos of the Communion or Confirmation, but then again, no one had them at that time.

My house below in Barrigone where I was brought up is now gone completely. There were three or four houses all around the shore like it. That would have been across from Aughinish Island, right across the tide from it and down across the fields from Mount Pleasant graveyard.

I went down to look for it once and I did not even know the field where it was. I knew where the well was that we used draw water from, but it has all changed and is like a big prairie now. Machinery went in there, took the whole place out, took every thing, and it is all gone into one farm now.

During the time of the Second War, you wouldn't get much loaf bread then, except on the black market, a black market loaf it was called, and it would be beautiful. The ration books were out at the time also. My father was an asthmatic and he had to get strong tea, and so my mother would walk it into Askeaton for the tea for him. My sister Maureen was the pet in the house and she wouldn't drink cocoa, coffee or milk. We used to have to drink them, but she used to get the odd cup of tea in between.

I will always remember my mother walked in one day to the black market and to Mass beforehand. It was a bad winter's morning. Her brother was married to the sister of the woman who owned the market and when she called, the woman never offered her so much as a cup of tea after she walking in and down from Mass. And she was a woman that was supposed to be cured in Lourdes! But she never offered her a cup of tea and she had to walk out again, all the way from Askeaton.

In later years, my mother died of a heart attack. She had had heart palpitations already and one day she ran out of her tablets and when she got them back she was full of energy. So out she went up the hill after a turkey that had run off. I found her dead in the morning.

I used to go to see old people and look after them when I was young. This particular woman I went to, she reared my husband, because his mother died after he had been born, and that was where I met him. He came to visit his aunt and that was it. That was below at the house in Barrigone now.

We were married only twelve years when he died sudden in his sleep, up here in Kilbradran. I am here thirty-five years now. I have two boys, and a daughter who is in England nursing.

After that, my life had changed. I got out of all the cows, I got rid of my car and I got out of all the machinery. I did find it harder but, of course, I hadn't the work to do. I missed the routine of feeding the cows and feeding the calves and then I missed the car as well. The three children were no bother when they were young but they got a clout every time that they needed it. But you cannot clout them when they are grown up!

My son Johnny, the Lord have mercy on him, died also. It had a bad effect on me, of course, but I was able to handle it. From a religious point of view, I said that if his soul was saved I would get over the body part. However, when a person dies suddenly you are worried about the body part too.

The last Christmas he was alive was the best we ever had because it was the first Christmas that he was at home in a while, and my son-in-law and my grandchild, who was only six months old that time, were at home also. He brought presents and he was on the top of the world. That would be one Christmas that would stand out in my mind.

I like poems and poetry and write some too. I used to do them for my daughter Mary going to school, when she was in first and second class. I did lovely ones, she carried them to school, the teacher put them up on the wall, and I never saw them any more.

Here is one about my dog:

Ruby the dog is our family pet,
She is twelve years old and is very alert yet,
She knows when a stranger knocks at the door,
She barks very loudly as she cross the floor,
She is a great little watch dog although she is very small,
She had a large family, nine litter, in all,
They are all scattered now north, south, east and west,
Wherever her breed is they are only the best.
I did not tell you yet her colour is black.
She loves us to stroke her and brush her wee back,
She eats very little and drinks little water,
And always is loved by my sons and my daughter,
When she passes out,
It will be with great regret,
Because she is our one and only family pet

I did this one for Mary when she was in first class going to school. She got a prize for that as well.

I have a little dolly she is straight and tall,
I keep her in my room standing by the wall,
Her cheeks are rosy red and her eyes are blue,
I fixed her broken arm with a little bit of glue,
I like her very much and her hair is dark and long,
Some times she talks a bit and sings a little song,
If any thing should happen her, I would be very, very sad,
And all the dolls in Ireland would not even make me glad.

The others are more childish but I did a small one for the Third World, a place we should never forget:

The Third World is full of woe,
And that is where all our spare pennies should go.
To see people starve is a terrible scene,
You see it all on the television screen.
Some people scarcely have one full meal a day,
And here we throw good food away.
They needs lots of money to help themselves,
To grow their food and fill their shelves.
And we should pray to God each day,
To help the Third World in every way.

1931: First Edition of the Irish Press published.

In February 1952, King George VI died, aged only fifty-six, and is suceeded by his daughter, Queen Elizabeth II.
Her coronotion in June was broadcast to millions worldwide by television.

Margaret Noonan

My name is Margaret Noonan currently living at Ballintubbrid, Newcastle West, Co. Limerick and I was born on the 22nd of July 1947, in Athea, Co. Limerick.

I didn't live with my family, as my mother died when I was eleven months old. I was reared by an uncle and his wife and their two daughters in the countryside, about two miles from Newcastle West

I went to the National School in Killoughteen and stayed there until I had finished sixth class. I then went to the Technical School in Newcastle West and I spent three years there. We walked most of the time, but if we were lucky, we would meet somebody going to the creamery with a pony and a car, and we got a lift from them. We were always very choosy about which one we got a drive from, depending on whether they had a fast pony or a slow one!

The teachers were rough at the time compared to today's but I always found them ok. We had one male and two female teachers in the National School who were very good. I think the male teacher was harsher with the boys than he was with the girls. He did have some bamboo canes and we were always aware that if we stepped out of line we'd get a slap of them. I had great respect for the female teachers because they always made sure that you stood by the fire if you got wet coming to school. You always brought your lunch and your bottle of milk with you to school and they'd put it down by the fire to keep it warm.

They were not bad at all now in the Secondary school. I got on very well with them, but today, the youngsters don't have a whole lot of respect for the teachers. There isn't a lot of discipline but then, teachers can't say a whole lot to the children either.

Those times you had to learn an awful lot off by heart. Today, it seems to be that they haven't got the same curriculum at all. That time you had to learn your tables off by heart, you had to learn your spellings off by heart, you had to learn your poetry off by heart and you had to do a lot of essays. I rarely see the children today having catechisms or table books or learning their ABC's.

One of the biggest experiences of my childhood was when I had my appendix removed at eight years of age. I remember going into the doctor on a Sunday morning with a pain in my side but he said to go home, as he thought I was only messing and didn't want to go to school the following morning. But that evening they had to send for him again and I was taken into the Regional Hospital in Limerick, which was new at the time, and I had my appendix out the next morning. It was a big ordeal to be away from home because it was my first time away and my father cycled from Athea to Limerick to see me every Sunday.

After leaving school I worked in a shop in Newcastle West. The people were very nice and they had a shop, a filling station and car sales. There was a lot of business going on there and I stayed for five years until I got married. I think my pay was about thirty shillings a week, which would be one pound fifty in today's money. That sounds like little today but at that time it wasn't bad. I was also kept in the house, which made an awful difference.

I went back to work again for about twelve months after getting married and my husband and I lived in a flat in Newcastle West for about three years. We had seven in the family so it's quite a big family at today's rate of going. We didn't move very far as we're still living about a mile and half from Newcastle West and my husband worked in different jobs fairly close. He spent a lot of his years in a factory in Castlemahon and most of our family went to school in Killoughteen, the same as I did myself, and then they went on to Newcastle West.

The entertainment in those days was mainly dancing at ballrooms, and the Olympic Ballroom in Newcastle West was in full swing. We would have travelled to Limerick City to the 'Jetland', which was very popular at the time, Dromkeen, the 'Majestic' in Mallow, and Abbeyfeale. We normally went by car, usually four or five of us together. The money to go to dances that time was about four shillings but four shillings wouldn't buy you much today or wouldn't take you very far. We also went to the picture house in the town. The older people played cards in the houses and I can remember my uncle going to the neighbour's houses at night and so many of them would come to our house and play card games.

We didn't have a television for many years, just the radio. I remember 'Céilí House' on Saturday nights was a great favourite of the family and we also went to some céilís in the area. The music at the dances was very much the show band scene, mostly country and western. You had Brendan Bowyer, Joe Dolan, and all those. I don't think that the older people and the younger people would be interested in the same type of music back then. But like we are ourselves today, I don't think we'd sit down and listen to the modern music. We still go back to the country and western and listen to that.

I can remember the first time the electricity came into the house but it was quite a few years after that that we got the television. There was terrible excitement when the television came in and sure we didn't know what to make of it as youngsters, but it was very good. We had an awful lot more entertainment but normally, in our younger days, we were out around playing a lot and would hardly ever be inside. When we didn't have television we didn't understand what it was to be inside.

My childhood memories of Athea are of going on holidays there during the years I was going to school. I think that was the only communication I had with my two sisters and brother at the time. Barnagh would have been much quieter and to go out to Athea was completely different and a great thrill for me, as my uncle had a shop at the time and we used to give a hand there. He also had a hackney service and did construction work during the day. I made a lot of friends in Athea of my own age group and then my sisters knew a lot of youngsters there, even though there would have been a good gap in age between myself and my sisters, I being the youngest.

My uncle and his wife didn't have any family of their own but everybody called his wife "Auntie", and it was a house that people would go to before a dance or before they'd go to the pictures. They have since passed away, but one of my sisters who worked in the shop with my uncle now owns it. I really enjoyed my holidays there because there was a great community spirit and we used to go to the pictures there, and coming from the country, going to the village would make an awful difference to me in those times.

One big happening I remember was in 1963 when we went an to Athea for the Christmas holidays. We got an awful lot of snow while I was back there and as it happened, I couldn't return from there for about six weeks. My father lived away from the village, very high up near Abbeyfeale, a place called Coole West. There was only one tractor coming from there a couple of times a week to try and get supplies for everybody else in the area. After the six weeks, I remember going to my father's house with my aunt and my sister and it was unbelievable. They just had a walkway cut through the snow and it was like a wall on either side as you walked through it. It was just something you couldn't imagine happening. It had snowed for six weeks and had frozen over and it was just as solid as a wall. Of course, I was delighted with the extra holidays at the time as I couldn't get back to go there!

My father worked with farmers, mostly in his younger days, and then he went to England and spent a good few years there, I presume on the buildings. My brother is still living in the house but my sisters were in England at that time. Then my sister Mary came home and she bought the shop from my uncle, so they're all living still around Athea, now that my father has passed away. He's dead for the last three years and was eighty-seven when he died.

I think we didn't listen enough to the older people when they were alive because a lot of the old things that we'd like to know today we can't. We just didn't sit down, listen and ask the questions. I often speak to my sister-in-law today and she'd say "all the old people of that generation are gone, why didn't we ask them if we wanted to find out something?". So I suppose there are a lot of things buried with them that we will never be able to find out.

It is so much harder for young people today because things are very hectic and there is so much going on. There are lots of demands and lots of dangerous things out there, drugs and all, things which are hard for young people to try and avoid. They have more money and cars and can travel almost anywhere they want to go, but I think our days were happier when we didn't have those things and made our own entertainment.

January 1947: *David Bowie (Jones), singer/actor was born in London.*

June 1963: *President of the USA, John Fitzgerald Kennedy, pays an official visit to Ireland.*

Mary Hickey

I am Mary Hickey and I was born in 1904 into a parish called Rockchapel in County Cork. There were a lot of young-sters around where I grew up and lots of houses there, full of very honest people. My mother and father had a little farm with three cows. My father worked as a thatcher but really, he was a jack of all trades. I had three brothers and one sister but the whooping cough killed her.

I remember my school days well, and I can tell you that they were rough and ready. I did like school; well, there was a master there that was a bit rough and he had a strap in the school that he would use. An inspector used to come once a year. I think he used to inspect all the classes, both small and big. I never learned Irish though, as it had just started to come in when I left.

The only games I played were at school, being an only daughter at home. There was nothing going that time and you would be terribly well off if you could get a ball.

After I left school, they put me in a farmers place working. I was a servant girl and I did the usual housework, like baking bread, washing the ware, cleaning up the house, washing the floors, preparing the food for the din-ner, and I was also looking after the children. I had a hard time. The wages were bad of course, about a pound a month, and that was all that was going. I wouldn't have to be up too early, about half past six maybe, and you daren't talk of holidays! We worked Holy days and Sundays and every day of the week.

I had an aunt in Queenstown married to a sailor and I went up to her then. I was a boarder for a long time in a school in Cork, and I went on a job in the Mallow Road, outside of Cork city. It was while I was in school there that I remember seeing the first car in County Cork. I saw it one day when I was going to school, and it was an ambulance.

I was there for a long time and my mother, she was funny, she stayed nagging and nagging me until I went home. I worked on the farm at home for a while.

One evening I went to a dance six or seven miles away. They were friends of mine running it and I met a first cousin of mine that I didn't even know about. Of course, I was never left go anywhere as I was an only daughter. This cousin took me back to her home. Her mother was dead and I thought the way she was living was miserable compared to what I had but still, I liked it and decided to live with her for a while.

I went from there to Newcastle West and stayed with another cousin of mine. They were hiring boys and girls at the hiring fair in the Square at the time and I was hired by a farmer and ended up down in Adare and that was my residence then for a while. One good thing was that I met my husband there. He was born in 1902, and together we had nine children - six girls and three boys.

The only remembrance I have of Christmas, and it's God's honest truth, is a loaf of bread and a pot of jam. We only heard of presents for Christmas!

There was a holy well near to us called St. Kieran's, in Kilmacow. You made the pattern day yourself in the month of September but there was a special day, the 9th of September, that you went to get cured. The crowds would vary all day long coming up through the fields as it was inside in the heart of a field. People travelled on bicycle and on foot and, very rarely, by car.

There would be big crowds in the house for the wakes. I remember when my grandfather died, the house was full and the rosary was said at twelve o'clock and they would cover the mirrors. The remains would then be taken to the church. They would spend the night in the church and would have Mass in the morning and at two o' clock, I think, the funeral would start and they would be taken to the church yard.

I had stories about the Famine but I have them forgotten now. You must remember, I was ninety-six last September (2000). I remember the 1914 and the 1918 Wars. I was not very interested in the 1914 War but I'll tell you, we suffered in the 1918 one. The Black and Tans one, I mean. They were death down on houses where there was a man or a couple of men hiding, and they used to take them out and shoot them. I had a brother in the war and he did jail. He was a member of the IRA and he broke out of the jail he was in, in Cork. I remember the Civil War too, and during it and the Tan War we had nothing to eat but old black bread. I remember Michael Collins and Eamon De Valera, who lived in Bruree near us, but I never met any of them. At the time of the rations in World War Two, we would get a piece of black bread and if you were lucky enough, you might be able to get potatoes.

We had a harder life than they have now because we were only children when we were put out footing turf, forking it, saving hay, and doing all sorts of men's work. The only machinery that was there was a scythe, and my father, the Lord have Mercy on him, used to mow the hay and he not even having a real scythe. It was a reap, like a long stick and a blade out of it at the end and it edged to cut the hay. It was terrible hard work for any one.

I was living at my last address a long time and it was there that I reared my family and I spent all my married life there. I went through many wars and I went through an awful lot of trouble, like burying four daughters with cancer. I am a grandmother to DJ Carey, the Kilkenny Hurler, and I saw him before one of his big matches this year. In fact, he is my first grand-child but no, he is not the favourite!

June 1959: *Eamon De Valera is elected President of Ireland.*

1999: *The popular sitcom, Father Ted, is the most watched programme on Network 2 television, with an average of 928,000 tuning in per episode.*

Mary O'Connor

My name is Mary O'Connor, now at St. Anne's Nursing Home, Dromcolliher, Co. Limerick, but I was born in Kanturk, Co. Cork and I am a native of Kilberra, Freemount, Charelville, Co. Cork. My mother and father were both farmers.

I went to Freemount National School in 1946 and I was very happy going there. I liked the teachers and I remember getting my First Holy Communion and Confirmation. I loved getting the holidays, but would be glad to go back again when it opened. From that, I went to the Tech. in Kanturk for a year, before going to the Convent in Dromcolliher, where I stayed with my aunt in Dromina. I got tired of that and I decided to stay at home with my mother and went to Kanturk School for another twelve months, and after that I got married. We used to walk to school everyday unless the weather was wet, and when it was, we would be brought there in the horse and trap. We used to play hide and seek and Blind Man's Buff, the one with the scarf tied around your eyes, when we were young.

I worked outside on the farm as a housewife and I loved it. I couldn't do anything else. It was a long day from half past seven in the morning until the cows would be milked at night, but we had plenty of help. It was a long day, but the way it was, we didn't take any notice of it, we were happy. We always got the days of the threshing off from the Master at school, Lord have mercy on him. We always got that day or two off, whatever we would have at the time. Farming today is better because you have more equipment and more machinery to help, but we had none of them things in my day, it was making windes of hay and binding the corn, which they don't do today.

The dances in the old days were great. We had an old practice dance in Freemount every Sunday night, and then you would have a big dance during the week somewhere. In those days, I think, for a dance until two o'clock in the morning, it was only five shillings. The farmer dance in Charleville used to be a pound but there would be a meal included in that. They used to have the teacher dance here in Dromcolliher and the creamery staff dance too, and I think it was twelve and six pence for them but I am sure we used to get a meal with that too.

I think I was married when the television came in. I remember I used to like the "Riordan's" and today, I also like "Fame and Fortune", but I don't ever watch "Coronation Street" or "Fair City" or any of those.

Religion back in my day was very important. You would have to fast from twelve o'clock the night before to receive Holy Communion, but if you didn't fast, you couldn't receive the bread. Before going to mass on Sunday morning you would have to milk a ban of cows or wash tankards. Usually, the first Sunday of every month all the women would be for Holy Communion and the second Sunday all the men would be for it. It was as important as the rosary to the people that time. At home, I think the rosary was said every night from October to May.

On St. Patrick's night, you could go dancing. On Good Friday and Ash Wednesday, you weren't allowed to eat any meat, because that would be wrong. Christmas was always grand with us and as we got older, we got toys.

There were no funeral parlours at the time, so the dead person would be waked in the house. They'd go to the church from the house and they would be buried the following day at two o'clock, after Mass in the morning.

I got married to my husband Dan, Lord have mercy on him, early in 1960. We were married in Freemount and Dan's first cousin the priest married us. It was around nine or half past in the morning that we got married and after that we went for a meal to the Central Hotel in Mallow and it was lovely. I think there was a dance until four or five o'clock in the evening, then there was more tea and cake, and after that we went away. It was just grand and there was no commotion like now. I mean, they have videos and pictures and all sorts of things now.

We had six children before Dan died on the 13th of February 1997. My eldest child was born in November 1960 and the youngest was born in 1969. I have two boys and a girl married. One of the girls is a receptionist in the Great Southern Hotel in Killarney and the other one is travelling for our lives in "Mallow Insurance" and comes home at night. My other son is at home running the farm.

Many changes have come in farming. Of course, you had plenty of milkers, plenty of help back then, but today, one man can milk a ban of cows on his own. I think the farmers are well off today. They might say they aren't, but I think they are. However, I think the farmers were happier back in the old days, but I'd say there is plenty of money in circulation today to keep them happy.

1946: Bord na Mona was established to develop the country's vast resources of peat.

1960: Future Irish goalkeeper Packie Bonner is born in Co. Donegal.

Michael Nolan

Turf Cutting and Lime Burning

The first stage in the process of cutting turf would be to edge your sleán, your hay-knife and your spade. You would then have to walk it about a mile and a half to the bog and you'd have plenty sweat up by the time you'd arrive!

The next stage is called "stripping". You'd put a cut along the length of the bank, whatever length the bank would be; it might be sixty yards, it might be eighty yards or the whole bank if it was only a one-sod bog. If it was a one-sod bog, you'd have to put the farthest-out cut out four feet to get enough turf out of the bank and this might be about one hundred and sixty yards long. There would be at least three of them in the width of the bank where you'd be cutting and you'd have to cross-cut it at the end of every foot, because if you cut the stripping sods too long, you couldn't throw them off as they'd be too heavy.

The next thing you'd have to handle then is your spade, and you would only be a half an hour at it when you'd find the palm of your hand getting very hot from the handle! There wasn't any fun in it at all. When you'd have it stripped then, you'd have get your sleán and you'd have to have a fellow taking it out of the bog-hole, up on to the bank. There would have to be another fellow outside to spread it.

It would take you about half a day to strip it anyway, after it taking you half a day to mark it with the hay knife, one hundred and sixty yards along the bank at four feet wide and that was a day almost gone before you'd do any cutting!

Cutting

The following morning you'd carry on where you left off and you'd have to have two more fellows with you, that's if you weren't able to spread the turf at both sides left and right. If the place was dry at both sides, you'd have to have three men; the sleán man, a fellow for throwing out the sods, and the lad spreading outside at the end. It would be there then, all depending on the weather, for a while before you'd foot it.

Footing

If you got fine weather you could foot it after five or six days. Some people used to turn it with pikes and you might only have to foot it once if you got the weather. It would have to have at least three weeks to a month of fine weather before you could draw it in as it wouldn't be seasoned or fit enough to make a fire.

When footing, you could put seven or eight or nine sods together if you were able. By turning the sods you would dry at least two sides of the turf before it was footed. You'd put two or three sods standing on ends to make a tripod and you could build six, seven or eight sods up then. After a fortnight, if some of it was after falling, you'd build them up again.

The turf was box footed if the weather was bad. You'd throw two sods on the ground, two more up on them and you'd cross them and then do the same again until there was about four, six or eight together. When they'd dry out, the top four sods would be fairly dry and you could put those four standing and put four more in between them and a sod on top. So that would be about nine sods in a rick. And that's the box footing, but you'd have nothing to do if the good weather didn't come.

Bringing home the Turf

Sometimes there was second footing to go through it to make sure that it was dry and you would make the stooks bigger and leave them there for a week or ten days again. Next came the horse and rail. It used to be horses and rails that were there that time but it all depended on if you could carry them into the bog. If you had high bog you'd have to get a donkey to bring it out, for the horse would get bogged down there.

The bogs would have to be dry but there were some bogs that you couldn't go into at all with a horse. In more places, if the weather was anyway dry at all, you could work away and have it drawn in a couple of days. You'd get about ten rails of turf out from eighty yards and twenty rails of turf out from the one hundred and sixty yards. The ten rails of turf would be called a quarter of turf.

There was better quality turf in different parts of the bog, and then there are bogs that even the top sod would be black and heavy. There is a bog out near Ballydesmond and this fellow cut it with the machine about seven or eight or ten years ago. He drew it home and put it into his shed and didn't use it at all that year. The following year he had to draw it out again and it fell apart like hot lime. It was too black, there wasn't enough of the fibre through it to keep it together.

War Years

We haven't sold turf for years now but we had some amount of it going during the Second World War, on account of there being no coal. The County Council and many other companies were cutting it that time and men came here from near and far, some came all the way from Cobh, to cut it. When they came first, there was about forty or fifty men there and any one of them had never see a bog. The first couple of nights they were in tents above and the most desperate deluge of rain came. They were lying on plastic sheets on the ground and the next thing, the water came down the field and it drowned what was on them!

The army came out to places cutting as well, but sure they'd ate more than they were worth! They were helping with the cutting because there weren't enough men left in a lot of places. Many people at the time hadn't enough food, as you'd only get about four and a half ounces of flour with the rationing, and I'll tell you, you wouldn't cut too much turf at all with small rations.

The Popes brothers were coming all the way from Cork City to here and would take away five to six tons of turf in a load. However, they burst nearly every bog road in the country as the roads were so bad that time and weren't able to keep up the pressure of the load. Then when the frost would come, the turf would be stuck together and they used to say "*First we quarried it and then we carried it*". When they'd arrive down around Mallow or further down to Fermoy, the water would be inclined to leave the turf and some poor old woman or man there that would be expecting to have a fire for the winter but would have only bags of water running out of the shed wherever they put in the turf!

So that was the turf cutting process - stripping the bog in the middle of April and start cutting out the turf some time in May, if the weather was anyway fair. June and July were the two good months for drying it and you might get a good August that you might be able to pick up a share of it.

Lime Burning

The limekiln was a different thing again. For turf to fire the kiln, you'd have to fall in at the stripping of the bog again for them and dry the turf, but it would have to be black muddy turf to put up the right heat to burn the lime. The drawing of the limestone was worse than the turf, as you'd have to go ten or twelve miles to the nearest quarry to get it. That's what it was from here over to Taur anyway.

You'd have to load the stone with the help of plenty men and even though there were three or four men quarrying over there, you'd still have to carry your own men to load it into the horse and cars. Of course, it was very heavy and a ton of stone was all that a horse could bring. When they were coming out of the quarries they were only able to bring out a half load until they came to the top of the road, then they'd have to take off all the stones by hand, go back down for the second half of the load and load up the whole lot again at the top of the road!

There would be maybe three horses together, you see, for the big rocks. They couldn't bring the really big rocks, they'd have to be broken up inside in the quarry and there was a special way for breaking it. It had to be sliced for it to burn in the kiln, as round lumps of stone wouldn't burn through at all.

To start off the burning, a fire had to be started in the kiln with maybe a couple horse rails of turf to start off with. A layer of stone was put about nine inches high on top of the fire, and when it would go down a little bit you'd have to fill in another foot of turf on top of that and then fill more stones into it again, and so on. When the lime would be coming down below to the bottom of the kiln it had to be taken out with a shovel and thrown back from you. When it would leave the kiln it would be kind of an ashy colour, depending on the kind of turf you had, and when it would melt then it would turn into a mostly off-white powder.

When you'd be drawing it away from the kiln after it been burned you'd have to leave it in the field, maybe two or three buckets of it together in a little heap. It would be like soft gravel but the first bit of rain that would come then would melt it and it would turn into lime then. But if you broke the stone wrong or if you didn't know how to throw it into the kiln, it would all turn out half burned and you'd have to be picking pieces of limestone off of the field to try to burn them again.

The length of time it took to dissolve in the field would all depend on how much rain it would get after going out, but even if it got no rain you'd hear the piece on the ground sizzling away. If you threw water into some of it for whitewashing and didn't look out for yourself it would burn the hand of you.

They used throw that on the land instead of manure, as there was no nitrogen or anything there that time, only the lime. It improved the place greatly, especially around here in the mountain areas, but I suppose they used use it down in the good places too.

When we were going to school in the morning, you would see the big plume of smoke from the kilns crossing east or west, whichever way the wind was blowing, and there was a most terrible thick, pure white smoke and a desperate smell out of it too. We'd see it rolling away along and often spent ages watching it cross the countryside.

I'd say Tom Welsh was the last one to burn lime around here about 1955. He was a young fellow at the time and he carried my father down to show him how to burn it. My father got a fierce land with the breaking of the stones because he never thought that it was such a big job. They had about half a butt of stones broken when they started to burn and Tom wasn't able to break the stones fast enough for the fire. He had to get a couple of fellows to help him to slice the stones and they had great fun at Tom when the fire started coming at him and he had no stones to throw into it. I'll tell, you he went for the ground after that!

During the Melbourne Olympics of 1956, Irishman Ronnie Delaney wins gold in the 1,500m. Ireland picked up a further four medals in the boxing, with Fred Tiedt (silver), Freddie Gilroy, John Caldwell and Tony Bryne (all securing bronze medals).

Mary Robinson was born in 1944 and went on to become President of Ireland. She is currently UN High Commissioner of Human Rights.

Mike & Mary O'Donnell
Coopering, Dressmaking and Teaching

My name is Michael O'Donnell of New Street, Abbeyfeale. I was born right here in this house. I had four sisters; Ann-Marie, Rose, who taught in Dromtrasna but is passed on now, Delia in Adare and Mary, who taught as well, in the Boys School in Dromtrasna. Previous to that she was in Dunlavin in Wicklow.

My father was a cooper and my mother, before her marriage, spent thirteen and a half years at Eccleston's Drapery. She married my father who was a grocer as well as being cooper, and they carried on the shop together.

My grandfather, Michael O'Donnell, of Church Street Abbeyfeale, started the coopering in 1865. It was at the back of the square then, and the building was known as the "shed", and it is still there to this day. As well as being a workshop it was used as the forge and the creamery and was a great meeting place. Later he was joined by three of his sons - Michael, who was known as "Squire", Tom, and my father, Bill, and the four of them worked together for a good many years until 1925. By then my grandfather and my uncle 'Squire' had died and my uncle Tom had emigrated to New York, and it was left then to my father. He moved the workshop down here to New Street and continued to work as a cooper until his death in 1949.

It was a hard trade to learn but once they got it, it was like child's play. They loved it and my father was never happy only when he was coopering. They had only the four of them as they never took on any apprentices but it finished with my father's death in 1949.

They made the butter barrels, the ones on a stand, which would take two people to churn. They also made the firkins for transporting butter, which were in great demand and were nearly bought on a weekly basis. The butter was packed into those, they were sold in the square and then taken to Cork by special men called "car men".

Every couple of weeks they went to the docks in Limerick for the wood because Abbeyfeale was very small at the time and if you wanted anything, you had to go to Limerick for it. It would be oak wood that was used for the butter barrels and also red deal. White deal would be too soft for the butter barrels, and they were very exact about the firkins because food and butter were going into them. Also, they used to make what they called meat barrels for farmers who were killing pigs, and the farmers were very careful that they wouldn't use those barrels for anything but for curing the bacon. Then you had the ordinary tubs and barrels for collecting water, washing clothes, and for feeding cattle. The pecks were for feeding pigs and they would be about a foot high and lower still for the bonamhs.

When they were making the barrels they had iron hoops that they put on first, to hold the staves in place, and then when they had the barrel all ready, they tipped them off one by one and replaced them with the galvanised hoops. The iron ones were part of the equipment and were only to hold the barrel together. Of course, they had to cut them off a roll and they had to be riveted to the barrel. There was no distinction between the people that bought them. Everybody would buy the barrels - if you wanted a wash tub, you would come and tell him what size you wanted, or you might have a couple of bonamhs and wanted a peck to feed them. It was everybody and anybody.

The items were all different prices but I remember quite clearly that a big wash tub was six shillings and six pence. That was considered a lot of money, considering that to hire a man that time to work the meadow or the garden was ten shillings a day, so six and six was a big outlay.

As far as I know, my grandfather was the first in the line of coopers in the family and I think it was in Knocknagoshel that he learned his trade, around 1860. There is an anvil here, hundreds of years old, given by that family of coopers to my grandfather in remembrance of some old man, and my father was always watching it making sure that anything didn't happen it. Of course, the anvil was made by a smith but nearly all of the rest of the tools were hand made. All the ones here were made before 1865, wherever he brought them from.

By 1949, business had died out except that people would come in to have hoops put on a barrel and it was more or less obliging them my father was. Then, it faded out completely.

In my mother's family there were four of her sisters that were dressmakers; Elizabeth, Bridget, Mary Ellen and Anastasia. Anastasia served her apprenticeship with a Mrs. Benson in Newcastle West. There was a fee to be paid but you were kept in the house and fed. I don't know whether she got any few bob pocket money or not but she stayed with the Bensons for three years, and they were tiptop dressmakers. You didn't just go to anybody to learn a trade, and most of dressmakers had to be good. My aunt, Mary Ellen Gahan, served her apprenticeship with a Miss Burke in the square in Abbeyfeale, where the 'Cellar Bar' is now. When she was finished, Anastasia and herself set up themselves in New Street. Then two of their other sisters, Elizabeth and Bridget, served their apprenticeship with them. So you had the four Gahan sisters together and later they took on apprentices as well. It was big business and coming up to Shrovetime, it was very busy altogether as they'd be all getting married and looking for costumes and what not.

Another busy time was before the Listowel races, as they'd be all wanting new style, and I often heard my mother, God rest her, saying that her sisters, not the apprentices, would stay up at night with candles as well as with lamps, trying to get the items finished. As well as the apprentices they took on, they had three trained and qualified dressmakers also. Mary Teresa Spears was from Manorhamilton up in Leitrim, Cathy Coonihan came from Mallow in Cork and Margaret Delaney was down from the Midlands. It will just tell you all the business that was going on. Some of the apprentices that were there at different times were Nell Carroll, Main street; Nora Broderick, Main street; Lizzie Collins, Bridge street; Liz Butler, Athea and Maggie Stack of Tarbert. They all stayed at Gahan's and my grandmother had to feed and look after the lot!

Everything they had and made was of good quality and I remember when we would buy something in Limerick and bring it home, my mother would turn it inside-out and say, "look at the way that is finished!" You know, checking out the over-edging in the seams and all the rest of it.

My father's first wife was a dressmaker as well. She was Katie Cahill from Inse Bán, and she was dressmaking from 1905 to 1926. She served her apprenticeship with Liz Wright of New Street in Abbeyfeale. She got friendly with my father, Bill O'Donnell, they married, and he lived with her in the town for a few years. They built this house here and he was coopering, she was dressmaking, they had the shop going together and they did a roaring trade.

She had a whole lot of girls dressmaking with her, and so it continued until her death. She had Rita Collins, the Square; Mary Ann Noonan, the Square; Eileen Ahern, Main Street; Jo Murphy, Bridge Street; Jo Moloney, Church Street; Mary Foley, the Hill; Nell Doody, Kilkinlea; Margaret Doherty, Newcastlewest; Nellie Sheehan, Mountcollins; Kate Kerins, Knocknagoshel; Annie McAuliffe, Knocknagoshel; Brid O'Connor, Knocknagoshel, Nora Brown, Knocknagoshel and Mary Sweeney of

Listowel.

For all the dressmaking that was going on in the house, two of the sisters decided to become teachers. But they loved it all the same, isn't that right, Mary? (Mary, his sister, is sitting by his side).

I loved teaching alright and I wish I could start all over again, but thanks be to God I am finished with the Department and all that bookwork, rules and regulations. If I could just lock myself into the room with my infants, I would be happy all day long. It's funny but when you would be involved with children you wouldn't even think of the time.

Teaching has changed a lot from when I was at it. What I don't like is when I meet teachers and they say to me that I am lucky to be finished with it. I think it would be very ungrateful of me to say that I'm glad to be finished with it because I had a great time but apparently things aren't as nice now as they used to be. There is no discipline and you can't look at them let alone lay a hand on them. I heard a story lately of a girl who was only obliging a friend by keeping an eye on her children and they were really getting out of hand. She said to the oldest one, who would be in fifth class maybe, "if you don't behave yourself I'll hammer you". "You can't" he said, "I'll ring Childline". She said, "you don't know the number" and he replied "I'll get it in the directory". Now that is a big change from my time. (Micheal agrees with her and carries on....)

The place was full of animals in the old days. Most of the houses, except where there would be maybe one of the guards or a banker, kept their own cow. Where else were they going to get milk that time. We kept the cow back in Willie Creagh's, where the football field is here now, and the rent from November to about February was four pounds and ten shillings for a cow, and for the pony it was five pounds. When we used to get the cow she'd be in-calf, and you hadn't a hope of getting milk from her, and there was no condensed milk or powdered milk or any such thing. Sometimes when I'd go back to bring home the cow I might have to bring fourteen or fifteen of them with me, but often the cows used to go home themselves. That is God's truth, and our cow used to stand outside in the road and would be bellowing at the door until some one of us would notice that she was there, so then we'd hop out, put our hand on her and walk her around and up the back of the house.

During the war there was compulsory tillage and the farmers had to have so much of the land under tillage. They wouldn't want it all so what they used to do was rent a half or quarter acre for planting potatoes or turnips. It only cost a pound to rent, that was all it was I'd say. All during the War, at the back of Creagh's, we had our garden with a few ridges of the early potatoes, carrots, parsnips, peas, and beans and of course the cabbage. You had to have the cabbage.

We bought the eggs from Castlemahon, all packed in a case and there was a regular docket book with three duplicates in there with them. One docket was put around the last egg with your name and address on it and the amount of eggs, one would be left in the book, and you got the third just in case there would be anything wrong with the eggs. There was thirty dozen in each box, divided down the middle with fifteen trays at either side. We bought them from Castlemahon and then we sold a certain amount of them on over the counter. We also bought the butter from them, but the butter in those days was packed in big boxes and my father kept me in for the half day, which I loved of course, and we'd load up the boxes, take them to the train station and send them back to Slattery's in Tralee on the passenger and goods train.

The women were always involved with the butter, the eggs and the fowl, and they would bring them into town and the men would help them with them, but the butter and the egg money was belonging to the women. A lot of the men sold cattle and they went straight to the bank with the cattle money, but faith, the women were well to do too! If the women were any good at all they could make a fine living with fowl, eggs and butter. They also took great pride in the cloths they would have around the butter. They used to be flour bags but they would be as white as snow. It sort of showed the good housekeeper the woman was. They were very hygienic, I'll say that for the whole lot of them, and there will never be butter like the farmers' butter.

I remember coming in from school and you wouldn't have a hope of getting a bite to eat because there would be always people drinking tea in the place. People didn't have very much money but they had enough and there was no such thing as being hungry. I would say we were comfortable, but not rich. My mother always held that the shop was great because number one with her was to feed the family, and at least you had everything at cost price. You would never be hungry while you had the shop and she loved it. We never had a complaint about anything and the customers were her friends and they helped each other through sickness, death, and everything else.

It was mainly groceries we sold in the shop but we had light hardware also, like buckets, brushes of all kinds, cups and saucers, brown tea pots and the aluminium ones, saucepans and all that kind of thing. In the springtime, we used to sell the bluestone and washing soda for spraying the gardens for the blight. You could say that you could get a bit of everything here. Often that shop door was open until half past ten or eleven at night and it could happen that at eleven there would be a knock at the door for a loaf of bread or somebody would have forgotten to get butter but you wouldn't take a bit of notice.

The place was full of good characters. We used to have a fellow coming from Newcastle, his name was Carr, and he used to have camphor, tie pins and safety pins and the like, and he also used to have ballads. They printed the words of a song on a sheet of paper and they were a penny each. We would be mad to get them and when we would see him coming, we used to ask my father to buy a ballad for us. He used to sell all these and more. People used to give him more than the value, but he wasn't begging by any means, and he was a very nice man.

We had a town crier as well, a bell man, called Paddy Broderick, but everybody called him "Sos". He used to go around announcing the upcoming things, like a fair or a circus coming to town. There used be pictures too, the silent ones, up at Tobins. At that time, the picture would be flashed on the screen and you would hear them reading out the text for it, but we thought it was wonderful. We would be often having our supper and the door would be open and you would hear "Sos" with the bell and he walking in the middle of the road going like this: *"Tonight up at the Abbey Hall a picture,* (or was it a play?), *entitled* **'Murder in the Red Barn'**. *Doors open at half past seven, show commencing at eight thirty sharp",* and this would go on and on. On the fair day, someone might lose a heifer or a cow and 'Sos' would be around of course, calling out, if anyone had seen it, and he would get a few bob for it. Supposing you had hay to sell, well after last Mass, 'Sos' would be above in front of the church and saying so-and-so has so many acres of hay and all the rest of it. It would be first quality advertising.

The big fair days in Abbeyfeale were the 29th June and the 24th September and they were days you were in from school. The square would be covered with cattle and they having horns like the bars of a bike and the cow dung was something else. There were stalls above in the street with women selling second-hand clothes and more of them would have the chinaware and ornaments, and more of them would have fancy buns.

I can remember the sandals and the squelching through cow dung and afterwards the sandals were never the same again, they would be as hard as a rock after the cow dung, but it was worth it. We'd meet people that knew us and they would give us sixpence or a few coppers and you made a bit as well. The eating houses in the arcade used to do a roaring trade. Nobody went into Leen's Hotel except if you were a millionaire.

Different entertaining people used to be there. There was an old fellow that used to come from Newcastle and he used to sit on a block and he had a long board with a doll at the end of it and while he'd be humming away, the old doll would be dancing and people would throw in a few pence to him. There was another one and he had a pram with a bantam cock inside in it and a gramophone playing records to it but nobody took a bit of notice. They gave him the penny but they wouldn't give him more because they couldn't afford it.

There was no other way to make a living though unless you had land, a shop, a trade or you kept people in lodgings. A couple of pounds meant an awful lot and remember that the old age pension was only ten shillings. There was also the bit of dole money, which was twelve shillings for a single man at the end of the thirties, but people hated going for it.

It was a very happy life that I have lived up 'till to now, and I could, like Mary and the teaching, say that I was very happy with my job. I stayed out of national school, and a couple of years afterwards I was half-sorry that I didn't stay on but then I was very happy in what I was doing. I retired from the shop at Christmas of 1997. It was time I suppose, but I was only sixty-six. I had a total knee-joint replacement that was a complete success. But sadly, the days of the small shops are over and it had reached a stage when you wouldn't sell a loaf of bread. It's a sad thing to say but I buried the most of my customers, as all the old crowd that we knew died, but from time to time their children would call back to us and we would get cards at Christmas.

> *1949: Twelve nations sign the North Atlantic Treaty, establishing NATO. Eire formally declared the Irish Republic.*

Edward Lynch

Edward Lynch is my name of the Square, Newcastle West, Co. Limerick. I was born in a rural parish in West Limerick called Coolcappa. My parents were born in Kilbraderan, Shanagolden where my sister-in-law is now, and my father was a farmer.

My earliest recollection in life is of my mother dying when I was very young, only a year old or so. After that, I remember being brought up with an old woman next door for a number of years. I think I thought for ages that she was my mother.

My first school was that of Creeves National School and after a number of years, when I got strong enough to cross the fields, I went up to Coolcappa. There was no bus at that time and we had to walk it to school and barefoot some days. From April to about November we were bare foot going to school with the bottle of milk and the couple of slices of bread for your lunch. I had some happy days and some tough days but I didn't really dislike it.

Later, I came to Newcastle West and went to St. Ita's Secondary School, as it was that time, and stayed there until the Leaving Cert. I had an uncle in Newcastle West, where we are now, who was in poor health so I filled in here at the bar with him. At that stage, I was nearly seventeen and I am here since.

At school, we had homework something similar to what is there now. In the secondary, we had two hours study at night, from six to eight, to do our lessons and we were supervised by one of the teachers. We went in at nine in the morning and we were out at three in the afternoon. There were only four teachers there that time, as the classes were small, but they were reasonably strict. It was a strap that they had to control us and you would get a belt of it across the back if you were out of line. To start off with in First Year, we had about fifteen in the class but by the time of the Inter Cert., it might be down to ten and by the time of the Leaving it might be eight. Some of the lads got good jobs and more of them went off to England working and it was an achievement to get to University that time. But Donnacha O'Malley opened the education for every one.

My first working experience, my first and last, as I said, was here in the bar. The fairs and markets in the town that time really depended on you and on a fair day morning you were up at five o'clock to have the door opened and you worked away until eight or nine that night. After that, the place would have to be cleaned up and the cow dung swept out of the place. In turn, the pub depended on markets, fairs and holidays to do business. Also, all pubs had a grocery counter too, which is now gone since the supermarkets took over.

I played a bit of hurling and football, but I didn't play for a local team because I wasn't good enough. Anyway, I hadn't much time because I was involved in the bar. Certain teams had certain pubs that they would tog-out in and go to the field from. Nowadays there are dressing rooms at the pitches but that time they used pubs to tog-out in and to get washed and dressed afterwards. It was hurling and football teams mainly but then the soccer started to come in during the early nineteen fifties. Before that there was a rugby team here going back years and I wouldn't remember when but they are here since.

Nash's dances were about the only thing in the line of entertainment there was. They had a dance hall in the larger of the Desmond Halls of the Square, though it burned down later. There were dance halls in every village that time. You had one in Castlemahon, Killeedy, Ardagh, Kilcoleman and there was one in Shanagolden that opened in the fifties. We often came out of the dance hall there and the lights would be out, pitch dark and you wouldn't hear a thing on the streets. If you could afford to go, you went once or twice a month or something like that. There were also two cinemas in town, Nash's and Latchford's, not that much but you had a variety of cinemas anyway.

The first television I think I saw was up in Cronin's here in the Square. We went up one night to see some sports personalities getting some awards. It was in black and white and was very snowy but we were happy with it and it was a big change.

The electricity came into where I was born and reared during the fifties and that made a huge difference to the country life. Now, you could light up the yard and the sheds, when before that you were going around with an old flash lamp or a lantern. It was a big change and it made it easier for people to work, with everything from milking machines to washing machines, cookers and all that sort of thing.

The holidays, church holidays, were very big days in town at that time. A lot of business was done though some people made it a point to go out of town on the holiday to do their shopping and you mightn't see them for a month then again, but certain holidays were very big days in this town.

St. Patrick's Day is still a big day in town. I can remember the parades well and apparently before my time there were big markets held here on Saint Patrick's Day but that died away too. I really remember May Eve, when we would be out shaking the holy water on the cattle, the crops and the land to keep away the piseogs long ago.

The 8th of December used to be a big day in town, but it's gone now too and like other holidays, died away. Businesses did very well on the 8th and in the later years it was the first day Santa Clause would appear in town and it was great for kids and parents alike.

Christmas was smaller that time because it wasn't celebrated in the same way as it is today, with all the wining and dining. We grew up during the War and the toys were very scarce. The Wrenboys were big at that time too and they traveled on foot across the fields from house to house in the country. They targeted pubs a good bit too because the crowds would attract them and they would get a few quid there when they finished playing. The tradition today is not as strong as it used to be. When I was young, we would go out as well but we wouldn't have a whole lot of music and we would just stay in the locality, make a few bob and go away home again. I would never sing, as I was poor at that.

I got very few holidays while I was here in the pub but I might get a day now and again to go to a race meeting or go to Listowel or something like that. I didn't particularly like Ballybunion, but I spent a good amount of time there all right. Some of us would pool together and get a drive, but before that, people cycled there. Most of the foreign travel in those days was done by boat and the plane didn't really come in until the sixties and seventies, but I do remember the flying boats coming into Foynes in the middle and late forties.

There was very little crime that time. The lights went out in the street at twelve at night and the place was pitch dark and you wouldn't hear a thing. If the lights went out at twelve o'clock now the place would be wrecked before morning!

I have lost track of most of my friends because, as you know, England was going well at the time and the world of lads went off there and America.

I got married at the age of twenty-five and I have two daughters and a son and they are all doing their own thing.

*Ireland has had numerous Academy Award winners, including Michele Burke, who won an Oscar in **1981** for the Best Make-Up in the film 'Quest for Fire', and went on to repeat that achievement in 1983 with another Oscar for Best Make-Up in 'Bram Stoker's Dracula'.*

*Rosemary Brown, better known as Dana, became Ireland's first Eurovision winner in **1970**, with the song 'All Kinds of Everything'.*

Nellie Hayes

My name is Nellie Hayes and I live in Shanagolden. I went to Shanagolden National School and it was lovely. The teachers were lovely and very good and it was Miss Sheehan that taught me, although there was a Mrs. Reidy there too who was a bit harsh.

My husband was going to school with me and I was going out with him for about six years. After we got married, we lived up in Mount David and we are here about twenty nine years. I have three boys and three girls and there aren't any of them more than three miles away from me.

My mother was born in Ballyhahill and my father in Mount David, near to the White River. My mother made every stitch we wore when we were young, for both boys and girls. She made my Confirmation frock and I remember it well, it being made from a lovely satin. She would take the old flour bags of long ago and boil them and bleach them and when they would come out they would be as white as snow. That way she never bought any sheets as she would sew two of them together and make sheets of them. You would not get any sheet as white as them today though. She died of old age when she was eighty-six. In the end, she had a very bad stomach and everything but she was a great woman.

My father was great man too and he could never sit down at all but he had to in the end, because his heart was at him. He'd do the road to Limerick twice a day with the horse and cart. He took pigs in with him each time but before he went, people gave him their orders for items and he'd bring out a load from the shops. The horse that my father had was very clever and all he had to do was just to give her a pull on the reins and she did the rest. He died in 1970, Lord have Mercy on him and give him the light of Heaven, and was only seventy-three.

It is embedded in your mind what your father and mother did because you would be so proud of them. People tell me that I am like my mother. I don't know whether I would be as good as her but I would be as clean as her and a fairly good old house keeper.

We are fine and near Knock Patrick here and you can go up the hill of a fine day and have a great view. There are masses there now these days and it is very well kept and well organized. Long ago the rosary was said there on Saint Patrick's Day and there was always a huge crowd there. It is well kept up there because there is a certain group who maintain it

After leaving school, I was sent into Limerick minding children, a job I got through a friend, and I stayed at it for about twelve months. Then I was working down at the hotel in Foynes, McOwens, who have gone since and it is the Fitzsimons' that are living there now. It was my job to make the beds and keep the place clean, do a bit of cooking and so on. I was there two years but I had to leave because I got a bad "flu".

Then I went to work for Doctor Agnes Nolan, who had a clinic on the Main Street of Foynes, and was there for six years until I got married. I was just doing her housework and answering her calls and I'd give her a hand if she wanted it. Those times there were no dental technicians around and while she would pull the teeth, I would stand beside to tend her. I left her then when I got married.

It was tough going when the children were young and growing up. Usually, I had to take two of them with me when I was going about my jobs. God help us, they were too young that time to know. One was of them was in the cot and the other would be lying down on a bit of a mattress. The rest of them then would be at school and when they came home, they would get their own little bit of food until I would get home and I would get the dinner then. Along with that, I would make four cakes of bread a night as there was no such thing as slice pans, and go out then and milk my five cows. It was no bother to me though.

There are a lot of big changes in Shanagolden. Down in the square, there are two funeral homes but before, one was a forge, although it is closed down now for twenty years or more. The Post Office used to be where the Credit Union is now. Nonie and Paddy Dillane had a shop and they used sell papers, groceries and oranges and all that kind of a thing. There was a man living here long ago and if he was alive now he would give you all the history of Shanagolden for years and years back. But nobody had the courage to get a copybook and a pencil and write down what that man was saying. He knew everything about Shanagolden, every whole thing until the day he died.

There were fairs and turkey markets here long ago as well. I remember my husband Jack selling heifers there and my mother would be selling turkeys and geese. It was great altogether to see all the horses and carts and all the railing grates and all with the turkeys. I think about November was the time of the year for the turkey market and it was for only the one day down in the square now around Cribbins'. It has stopped a good bit now, for over twenty years anyway. It's a pity though, as it brought great custom and everything to the village and it was a great get-together for people.

You would never hear anything bad coming out of Shanagolden. No one has anything bad to say to the next one and you can go and do your business and let the next one carry on whatever way they want to. I remember I had two E.S.B. men staying with me for a while at the house in Mount David. They were putting up the electricity poles and all that and they were very nice men. Afterwards, when they were leaving, they said that when they had been here a week they had two wives got and that it was the loveliest place that anybody had ever been to!

*Earthquake kills more than 50,000 people in Peru on **May 31st 1970**. The SDLP is formed by John Hume and other members from his party in that year also.*

Pat Dalton

I'm Pat Dalton and I was born in Dublin in the 1940's after the War. My mother was a district nurse and she worked in St. Ita's Hospital in Newcastle West for over thirty five years. My father had a business, a shop on Church Street, and we had the leather, the tacks and the rubbers that time for people to repair their own shoes, but we also had groceries and china.

I was late going to school, nearly five and a half, as I had a lot of sickness in my youth. I spent about a year and a half in the Convent and I then went to the Courtenay Boys School where I made my First Communion and Confirmation. After that, I went to St. Ita's Secondary School, where the Carnegie Library was and where a business complex is now. I did five years there and after my Leaving Certificate I did a commerce class; typing, short hand and book-keeping, and that's what I liked.

I didn't really like school as it was incomparable with school today. They love school today but I think we were terrorised. We had a couple of teachers and they were something, I assure you, that wouldn't be tolerated now. There was a couple of us that used to be kicked around the class and all that. It was something else, they were brutes.

Religion was a big thing with us and we always had the Diocesan examiner. So much of the day at school was taken up with religion and getting ready for his questions and there was a special day every May for an examination on Catechism and Liturgy. That time, the Bishop came once every three years but now he is coming every year as the classes are bigger and there are more in the schools. It's unfortunate that the wheel has turned and there aren't vocations like there used to be, because one of first persons you see when you come in to the world is the priest baptising you and when you are going out it's through the priest as well, and I think its necessary to have them.

I started my first job in 1964 and I worked in Herbertstown Creamery, in east Limerick. It was a co-operative creamery so we had groceries, drapery, hardware and a department store, but I was in the office. They had a very big business that time and had about eight lorries on the road supplying the farmers so we were kept very busy, but we had a half day every Thursday. I stayed in digs in the village of Herbertstown and felt it a big change to have come out of a big town and out into the country. But then I had an accident going to work one morning, a car crash, and I finished work there with the creamery. I moved back home after that.

When I came back home to Newcastle I was in hospital and was knocked out for eight months with a broken leg. The surgery wasn't perfect and they had to re-break my leg and reset it, so the accident caused me a lot of hardship. It took a long time to get back and the doctor advised me that I'd be better off working down here in town. I got a start with Jackie Ahern who had a big hardware store on Maiden Street. He had a big business going on there and I stayed about fifteen months.

Not long after, my father's health got poor so I had to stay at home with him. The last job I had was with Telecom Éireann as a night and Sunday telephone switchboard operator. I was there for fourteen years until, due to automation, it went automatic and I was made redundant. I often worked every second Sunday evening from six o'clock until eight o'clock in the morning. If I did seven nights night duty I'd have seven nights off, something similar to the nurses in the hospitals, but you really needed a week off after a week's night duty because your sleep was disrupted. To be fourteen years on night duty was a long time for your whole system.

The wages were quite good that time in Telecom. They were as good as what you'd get around in other jobs but they have gone up so much since. I got on fine with all the workers and once you did your work and minded what you were doing it was okay. The boss was a hard and a strict man but he was a good man to work for and when you wanted time off it was always given.

I have worked for most of my life and I always keep myself busy. You'd want a job today with the cost of living as it is. I was just lucky that I had my property and was able to rent it, but you'd want to be working or you couldn't exist. What you'd get in the social welfare wouldn't help at all, even after all your life stamping, and what you'd get in redundancy isn't much good either. I suppose when God gives you the health, it is your wealth.

I haven't worked now since 1987, but I do a lot of social work for the aged and the senior citizens and things like that. I started the Going Strong Club with Fr. Boyce but it broke up after about twelve years and unfortunately, it hasn't been the same since, but I have kept up the tours and outings. I am Chairperson of the Red Cross for the past two years and I have plenty to keep myself going.

I always liked music, and although I can't play an instrument, I do like singing. I'm in the church choir thirty or forty years, nearly since I was a child going to school, and we meet and practice every week. When we were small there was really only the cinemas, Latchford's and Nash's. There used be dances and ceilis in the Desmond Banqueting Hall that's now open to tourists and visitors. The Olympic Ballroom then came after that. There'd be three or four circuses going around too and they were a big event in those days but I think it was the television that really got rid of those circuses and road shows.

There were great old people around, like Major Tully, who was a great character. He lived down Maiden Street and he was a bit of a fortune teller. Josie Coffey was a great fortune teller in Maiden Street also and she died there a couple years ago. The old people believed in those things but now people wouldn't believe in it at all. There is a Madame Lisa, a clairvoyant, that's supposed to be good and she comes around to hotels and places once a month. The Culhanes were great characters and they had a shop on Bishop Street and you'd never be without a laugh when you went in there. They were two old women that never married and they were very generous. They had cats that used to take over the shop, jumping from the top shelf down to the bottom but they were great sport.

Church Street was the principal street for the fairs and there was a lot of eating houses here to feed people. The street here had Mrs Morrissey and Miss McDonagh with their houses and they'd be three or four days getting ready for the crowd that would be coming. The big stands would be down in the Square every month but the biggest fairs were on August 20th and December 10th. All the pubs would be full and it was good for everyone.

I have relations in the States and I was there two years ago, in Brooklyn, Washington and New Jersey, and it was very interesting. I wouldn't advise anybody to go to America unless they had relations there as it's very expensive. It's a marvellous experience to travel though and anyone should do some. I don't really like the heat so I'd never be a person for going on sun holidays and I wouldn't be able to stick it in June or July.

I'm fourteen years married on May 31st, 2001. May, my wife, is a hairdresser and had her own business but gave it up due to health reasons about two years ago, so she has the salon rented out now. We do bed and breakfast as well but there isn't many tourists this year, as the Foot and Mouth Disease didn't help the industry at all.

I am taking a tour to Lourdes soon and think it's the trip of a lifetime. There is something about it that's lovely. I have been to the other Marian shrines but Lourdes definitely sticks out. Fatima is lovely but you can't compare it to Lourdes. The people in Portugal are a lot poorer and it is not as commercialised but it is getting there. The message of Fatima from Our Lady is prayer and the way the world is going, we should all listen to Her.

1964: Ireland decides to send troops to serve with UN forces in Cyprus.

1987: National Lottery is launched in the Republic.

Patrick Fitzsimons

We used have great nights there in the home place long ago, above in Cnoc Pádraig. We used have a singsong and my mother, God be good to her, had a piano, and neighbours would come to hear her sing and play. If my father came home from Shanagolden, he'd sing for you too! He was a farmer.

It was all big families that time. There was seven of us there, eight of the Ryan's and there was eleven of the Danaher's.

I'd have been about six when I started going to school. There was a good crowd in my classroom, maybe fifteen or sixteen of us or thereabouts, of the same age. My brothers and sisters were going to school with me at the time too. But I had the bulk of it gone through when I was thirteen and a half.

I was never in secondary school but I'd have loved to have gone there at the age of twenty. I could retain all I liked at the age of twenty. I described it all to a great Garda sergeant here years ago, Sergeant Darby. He kept me below in the station one day, and as we drank bottles of stout, he asked me about my school days and as I was telling him about it, he said that late maturity can happen.

I was a slow learner going to school but I met the wrong people. There is a teacher here now at the local National school and she is teaching all the slow pupils, that's a gift in itself.

I have a small bit of Irish but it's very limited. If we were left alone I'd have learned a lot more going to school. I used like the bit of Irish – "Conas atá tú? Ta mé go han-mhaith, go raibh maith agat. Seachain do ghnó fein, tá eitleán insan spéir." That was all with Bean Uí hÓgain (Mrs Hogan). We'd have to recite all these phrases and write them down in English and in Irish… and if she heard another plane tomorrow, it was the same again.

But if you do a thorough job everything works out lovely. They are all talking about education in the world of today. The curriculum is all wrong. The teachers themselves will have to go back to school again and they will have to learn European languages. If two German girls or two German gentlemen walk in the door there and start speaking German and they ask us a question and we can't speak their language, aren't we in cloud cuckoo land? If you could converse with them it would be beautiful, but how can you learn with the thing inside in the corner, the television? They are watching programmes there not worth a ball of blue, whereas if you had a German or a Spanish speaking programme, they'd be making progress. The standard of education this minute is no better than it was a hundred years ago. All the intelligent people are like the last rose of summer, faded and gone.

Back in 1984, I took very ill and I was away in Barrington's Hospital for six or eight weeks. Prior to going to hospital I bought Denis O'Rourke's meadow of hay above, aftergrass and all, until the end of November. I went away to hospital in June and I didn't come home until the end of August. 1984 was a wonderful year, very warm and sunny and the crops was actually burned in the ground. The night I came home I came down here to Shanagolden and I met Breda Cahill and I asked her was her father around and she said no, that he was gone down to Tipperary. Will you give him the message, I said, when he'll come home in the morning that if he could call up to Fern hill to me, he might be able to cut the meadow of hay I bought above off of Denis O'Rourke and Breda said she would.

Donie never called that morning but I had the lock off the gate since the night before and when he passed up he just went away in himself and got started. I had Tommy Lenihan helping me with the cows and he remained with me while I was in hospital and he remained with me for three weeks after coming home from hospital. I called up to Donie afterwards and he had a good share cut and I came down to Tossie Cribbin's and I carried up "dannos" (Baby Power bottles) to him and left them inside above and Donie said to me before I left, "you needn't worry about the dinner or anything else for me, anyway Mary, my wife, will have the dinner ready because you have no one below, and when it comes to dinner time I'll go home and I'll ate and I'll come back again and I'll finish the meadow".

And that is exactly what happened. We brought home the hay. The hay was baled on Friday evening. It was cut on the Tuesday and it was baled by Friday evening. In all, thirty-four neighbours turned up to help us out and we had a night below in Tossie Cribbin's afterwards. Patsy Moroney here in Shanagolden then asked me to compose something about the saving of the hay in 1984. I told them I would and this is the way the recitation went:

It was a custom in old Ireland in the good old days gone by,
When Pat Fitzsimons in Fern Hill met with a problem
and on kind neighbours he could rely,
voluntary help it was forthcoming, until I got on my feet
and overcame my problem, be it in country or in street,
I thought the custom had faded but now I know I was wrong,
Since I lay ill in Barrington's hospital not feeling very strong,
Wondering how I would get around for to get the harvest done,
As each fine day was passing by brightly shone the sun,
What a pleasure and surprise to me when the kind neighbours came,
Soon all our hay Donie Cahill had cut down
sure they turned and they saved that same.
During the warm days that followed they worked with all their might,
From early morning through the day until the close of light,

'Til every sop was harvested and bound in bales so tight,
And stored in the barn to my hearts great delight,
While my name is Pat Fitzsimons their deeds I can't forget,
It's nice to know in Shanagolden and Knocknaboula,
We have kind neighbours yet who voluntary gives of their time,
Without rewards or gains and show that Christian spirit,
That the good Lord so ordained, May the good Lord reward them,
As indeed I know He will,
has He not said that not one good deed shall go Unknown to Him,
I hope that in His records on judgement day will be,
The names of those great men who came and saved our hay.

When I was younger, I was working above at home and also went away working for farmers then. It was twenty-eight pounds for the year, that was the wage at the first place I went to. I had a terrible working day. You'd start early and finish late every day of the week. On Sunday mornings you were out at the first spark of daylight. And in the summer time, you had to milk twenty cows and bring all the milk to the creamery below here, a good four Irish miles.

We had a great time in the bog too. There would be crowds of people going in those days and even through all the war years. Spa Hill bog we used to go to, if the weather was good, at the end of March and early April. The climate now is unreal compared to the weather at that time and you'd have all the turf home in early June.

I was working with a blacksmith and I was working with a stone cutter. Variety is the spice of life, they say. I stuck with them for a few months or as long as they'd want me. But I had great days with the blacksmith, the making of the shoe and the rising up of the horse's hooves, the burning of the hoof to get the shoe into it. It was Wilbert the blacksmith I was with, on the road as you go to Foynes.

You had the world of tradesmen here in bygone days. In this village alone you had nine different tradesmen between carpenters and all the whole lot. Jimmy Behan above here was a carpenter. John Joe Mulvihill was a harness maker, the best in the country to turn a horse's collar so that it wouldn't choke the horse. All that's gone now, along with people doing the thatching, like "the last rose of summer", faded and gone.

They said there was supposed to be a cure for warts on your hand if you came across a stone with a hollow and water in it; bless yourself three times with the water and the wart was supposed to go away. If you heard the clock ticking, that was a fairy and keep away from it. But they were great people with cures for ringworm and lots of things.

There are terrible changes in agriculture. It's all the big man now and the small person is ruled out altogether. The big farmers can go to the big stores and order twenty tons of artificial fertiliser and they'll get it and get time to pay for it because they are in a position to pay for it. The small person might want a couple of tons but they might have no money to pay for it and there is extra charge in it when you do go paying for it. The same with shops. The small shop is closed and the big ones are taking over. Supermarkets, they are domineering the whole lot. They can buy in bulk, work the money and make a quick profit. As they say, a light profit makes a heavy purse. But still they are not happy and they want to buy a whole chain of shops. As is the case with farming, they can continue on buying, get bigger all the time and they'll put an end to smaller holdings, which, at the end of the day, is not wholesome.

To go back then to what old Mrs. Kearney said, "Any of us had nothing but we shared nothing and we all had enough". Now, nobody has enough. They have five hundred this week; they want six hundred next week and shorter hours. There is a limit to all that, so far till they go no further. It will take time to do what I'm speaking about, it will take time. It is all speed and "I'm in a hurry", but, hurry died and lazy buried him.

What's all the hurry about? They are gone to a stage where they'd pass their mother in the road as if they haven't time to pick her up. Come out from Mass on Sunday and they are gone in three minutes. No one has time to say "Good morning" because they are gone. Long ago when you'd come out of the church in Robertstown, God be good to my father, we'd be talking to the neighbours for a half an hour or more. I would consider that a change.

I played one game of football as a young lad going to Foynes School. They were short one in the team and I didn't want to go down. My buddies knew I was good to run as I could go like a hare, but no way would I agree to go down. I was coming up by the incinerator and our teacher thought of a quick number to call me back. He had sweets and he gave them to my comrades and they followed me up to the incinerator and I like a fool stood to take a sweet and three of four of them came around me and they caught me and they dragged me down and into the school. The schoolmaster said to me, "before I slap you, will you go down and play with the team, they are short one". "No sir, I will not," I said. "I'm asking you again," he said. "No", I said "I don't want to go down to play at all". He got the holly rod and he gave me six cuts of the holly rod as hard as ever he could. "Will you go down now," he said. "All right so," I said finally.

We went away down anyway and we togged out below in the field as if it was an All- Ireland we were going to play. Anyway, the referee blew the whistle and threw up the ball. The boys made a drive and they got the ball and kicked it down towards me. I was in front of our own goalie and when I saw them all coming in on top of me, I turned around and scored a goal against our own goalie. I was called off the field on the spot and that finished it. It was the happiest day of my life. I didn't want to play at all and if they left me inside I'd have scored another one. I had that in my head.

I used to go to see my school pal playing, Bernard Madigan, also known as "The Bone" Madigan. I thought he was one of the best people that ever went in to play a match. They would meet great teams but they couldn't get the upper hand of The Bone. I saw him marking a Garda one day and the guard was six foot three and Bernie only five foot four or that way. He would go up over his man, spring clean into the air. He was fantastic. I also had an uncle here, John "Cinder" Mulvihill, the likes of who never went into a football field since. And with Jimmy Behan, the carpenter, they had a great team.

There wasn't a gate in the parish I couldn't vault over it. The reason was, well, just in order to get to the other side. I wasn't going to open the gate when I had the ability to go clean over it! We had some great outings robbing orchards. I went to school with a boy called Sean Heffernan, Tim Heffernan's son. Tim Heffernan was a shoemaker by profession and one of the greatest men that ever put on soles on anything. But there was an orchard, anyway, known as Fitzmaurice's. They had a wire fixed outside so that when you'd be coming in you'd touch it and the bell would ring inside in the kitchen. The dog would bark and they'd be out in a flash.

John Heffernan found out about the wire and the bell inside so he cut the wire. He had everything laid on and organised his group. I was with them. We had a couple of good half sack bags and I suppose we cleared out the orchard. They could never know how it was done. We enjoyed that evening and we ate apples for a good bit after that. All that type of devilment went on.

I used to go to the dances in Athea twice a week, Friday and Sunday night, on a good pony we had at home. I met a lovely girl one night in the Grange. Betty Broderick was her name, from Pilgrim Hill, Kilmorna. When we came out, I said to Betty, " I have the pony tied over in Bill Irwin's haybarn." He had a pub in Athea and we used drink there. I used to put the pony at the back gate and tie her on to the pillar of the barn and give her hay. We came out anyway and Betty's bike was flat out altogether." Come in with me," I said "and we'll harness up the pony and we'll put up the bike upon the car and I'll take you back to Kilmorna." which I did. So she said to me, "When you are going home now go down the short cut go to the double cottage". There is an old man living there and the salute he'd give you at that time was "God bless you", so they christened him "God bless you". So I came on and I did what Betty told me. I came on over to the double cottage that morning and the moon was shining bright and I went down into Leahy's yard in Mín an Easpuig and on home, It was getting on now and I was afraid they'd be up at home. I arrived with the pony anyway and there was no stir at home. It was getting on for five o' clock in the morning. I untackled the pony and I dried her with a cloth and I walked her up and down the avenue to what we used call Brian's gate, the dividing gate on the farms going to the cemetery. When I got the pony cooled down I put her into the house altogether then, in case she'd get cold, and I went in and I lit the Primus and put on the kettle. I started getting the cups and making a bit of noise and I went up stairs and I shouted to them, *"Are ye getting up at all today?"* letting on that I was all night at home through roguery. So they got up and ate the breakfast anyway and tackled up the pony. We used have to come over two miles to milk the cows like but we got through all that and they knew nothing! I had great nights behind in Athea dancing.

We used to come here to Shanagolden after the hall was built in 1950, and the crowds that would come here! The perspiration would be dropping down off the gilders overhead so you would think it was raining, as there would be over a thousand people inside in the hall.

The first television I ever saw was over at Cahill's in Croagh. A great illustration came on it that night about a man who thought he had a terrible cross in life. I couldn't say what year it was but it was in the sixties. But I don't have time for television today. I like the horse racing on television and I like a good clean game of football and I listen to Radio Galtee a lot. I so happened to get in above to St. Ita's Hospital in Newcastle West when I broke my hip in September 1999 and I got in by a pure stroke of luck. Geraldine Sexton was singing on the radio and you could waltz to the music, but who came up right in front of me at the door but the matron and two nurses. "God", says she "you are mad for music". "I love music matron", I said "and if I had the use of my hip I'd have you up and down the corridor there". So I used have lovely music above every night. Music when properly played makes the dumb animal stand in the field!

The first sea plane that came into Foynes was called the 'Caledonian'. We were only youngsters going to school and I remember that we had the privilege of being left off to see it. A group of us had to go back by the sea wall and the teacher was supervising us to see the plane. That was many a long day ago. I wouldn't be surprised if it was sixty one years ago.

Years ago, John Duffy brought a circus to Shanagolden. He said, one night, that you'd meet as big a ruffian in Shanagolden as you'd meet anywhere in the world and he was 100% correct in what he said. The circus was above in the Diamond field across from our gate and they broke what he had there one night and there was no need of it, quite unnecessary. They broke the wagons, the glass in the wagons and everything. Any type of black-guardism shouldn't be tolerated in any society and I wouldn't have much time for it. A peaceful co-existence between neighbours and nations is what's desired.

I'm glad I got the whooping cough, chicken pox and the measles in my youth because if you got them in advanced years it would be the cause of your death and there's not a vet in the country that would save you, never mind a doctor.

Dr. Agnes Nolan, she was very good, God be good to her. She went around the country doing calls at all times, doing sick calls and everything in the middle of the night under the cruellest of circumstances. Once she called into Paddy Purtill, a first cousin of my father's, one wet evening. The White River was flooded and the call had come to a house in a long passage so Paddy tackled the pony and put the seat up across from the guards in the car. Dr. Nolan sat up and they came down the passage and crossed the road and on in across the White River, as there was no bridge there at that time. She said to Paddy, "we'll be drowned!". "We won't", Paddy said, "The pony is used to the water", and the car was going this way and that with the power of the water. She went in, did her duty and came out and up to Purtill's yard again. You'd get nobody to go through that ordeal in the present day. She was a wonderful person.

There was a boy who'd have been years older than I who was a bit slow at school. The confirmation was coming up and they didn't want to leave him out of the class. I was put out of the class myself but I was put back again. The teacher told the Bishop that he was a bit slow at school and that on the day of the confirmation he was to ask him an easy question. They came up along anyway and the bishop said to him, "well, little boy, did anything strange happen at the death of our Lord?" The child looked up at him and said, "not to my knowledge Father!" Isn't it something I'd say myself this minute? What could I know about what happened at the death of our Lord? "The earth trembled the dead arose and appeared to many" was supposed to be the correct answer but his answer had more common sense attached to it. Where are you going with education when common sense is instinct enough? They thought the child was a fool but the child was brilliant.

All the older generation liked to celebrate. We'd be coming up then and we'd be asked to sing songs and all this and you'd join in. Old Mrs Kearney, God be good to her, was ninety-three when she died below in Dernish. I used to go down to visit her and she told me that in her young days there was nothing, but they shared the nothing and they all had enough. I thought it was a wonderful explanation of the way things were.

If you were short of tea and sugar, you could come over to my house, and if I wasn't there, you could take it away. If I was held up for a bit of bread or anything, I could go over to you. All that's changed now. The doors are locked and the fear of Christ is on them. They'd hardly open it to let in their sister except they knew her voice. I don't blame them, that's the world you are going into now. All the doors were open long ago, and you might get up in the morning and find an old travelling man and he snoring in the kitchen, having just walked in the door and lay down and slept away for the night. You'd make a cup of tea and get him going again for the road. I don't think that will ever again come back, not during my term of office anyway.

We used have great Christmases long ago, the same as God made the world out of nothing. When we were small, Santa came and you'd have all the excitement about what Santa had brought us before going off to Mass in the horse and trap on Christmas morning.

On St. Stephen's day, there would be all the Wren boys then, there would often be forty of them and it was a great tradition always. I used to go to the wren parties but I used never go out on the wren, but my brothers would all right. My brother Mick used to play the mouth organ and the piano. When he'd come home from the dances he'd start playing and my father and mother would be sleeping overhead the room and there'd be war then that morning. All the music he'd heard at the dance, he could retain it all and play it back on the piano. I love music myself but I can't play; if I could play I'd be gone on the road years ago.

In my youth, people used to come to the pattern day of St. Patrick's Well, above in our field on Knockpatrick, on St. Patrick's Day, and say rosaries and sing hymns. Then they'd continue up to the cemetery and sing going up and sing coming down. They used to come from everywhere; Loghill, Ballyhahill and Foynes, and all the Bog Line would be pickled with people walking or cycling, on donkey and car, on horse and trap. They would come in droves there. It was same below in Barrigone on the 15th of August, and St. Colman's in Kilcolman on the 29th October and they'd take the water home with them.

We were told you are not to eat any meat on Friday or anything like and we abided by that until we got older. As I grew older, I became wiser and I used to steal the meat of a Thursday and I'd have it on Friday above on Copse's hill by myself and I took no notice of anybody. I formed a religion of my own. I had my own way of thinking; pay my own debts, mind my own business, and fall out with nobody.

I worked in the bog during the Second World War and you'd get a half ounce of tea every Friday evening from Jo Jo Shannessy. I remember the clogs and then the timber boot. The clog was a terrible design but there was none better available than the boot. I wore them myself back then and it was a pity that some weren't preserved as they would be as good today as the day we got them. But as for the clogs of bygone days, they were terrible and you'd be better off barefoot!

All of my family went abroad working and I was the one that stayed at home. They all emigrated. I have a brother Willie in Australia, my brother John in New York; Ita, Nora and my brother Mick, God be good to him, went to England. All the neighbours went too, to England, Australia and everywhere. One even near Russia! They did any type of work to keep the show going. Wouldn't there be many an Irish man in a bad state only for England? The truth is bitter when 'tis told. All people got employment in England and got going when there was nothing in Holy old Ireland only your rosary beads, your Irish, your Catechism, and your hymns, all of which wasn't any good to you for a living. I knew neighbours that went to England, came home and they were great people and they sent home money and they built houses and got work locally and kept going.

I was six months short of forty years of age when I got married to Nora. She is from Clare and we met in Newport one night. We have three children; Nora, Martin, and Margaret who are grown up now. Martin was in Spain but is home again, Nora is in Holland and Margaret is in Dublin. They all went to Stella Maris School in Foynes. They had a superior life to mine and fair dues to them, they availed of it. Still, I'm not one bit sorry I put down my life. It's a long time off yet, but I might draw the two thousand pounds from the President later on, I'll make the best go I can for it anyway. They say for a fact that old soldiers never die, they only fade away and life is what you make it.

I'm addicted to poetry. Once I start learning to retain, it you might as well be talking to the wall as talking to me. I learned poetry going over to Danaher's for a load of gravel. I'd have a piece of paper there and I'd refer to it if I was beat to it but to commit poetry to memory is a nice thing. You could write poetry for me in your own handwriting or you could type it out altogether, but I could never learn that. I'd have to rewrite it myself and commit it to memory. My mother, God be good to her, was great as she was very well educated and I learned a lot from her.

What's the best way to keep young? Mix with young people but don't try to keep up with them. As they say, the two best cures in the doctor's book are a good laugh and a long sleep.

I'll be seventy-two in October 2001, please God, if I live for it. If my accident that I had in September happened in the back yard, I'd be growing the daisies by now. I'd be got a day or two after and it would be a case of "house private, no flowers", but my number wasn't up, it's as simple as that.

" 'Tis nice to know that somebody cares and keeps us well in mind,
To know that someone's thoughts of us are with effect and kind,
This message is sent with wishes warm and true,
To let you all know here in Shanagolden today,
That Pat Fitzsimons from Fern Hill cares and thinks a lot of you. "

1929: The Shannon Hydroelectric Scheme is officially opened.
1950: Dr. Noel Browns 'Mother and Child Scheme' announced.

Seán and Patsy Ryan – Shoemakers

The following is an extract taken from an interview with the Ryan brothers, Seán and Patsy, from Abbeyfeale, who were shoemakers in their time.

Interviewer: When and where were you born, Patsy?

Patsy: Here in New Street, Abbeyfeale in 1933. Myself and the brother there are twins.

Interviewer: Had you any other brothers and sisters?

Patsy: No, our mother died when we were fifteen months old. She was just twenty-nine.

Seán Ryan: Our aunt was minding us then up until we were nine, but then she died and we were scattered.

Patsy: I went to live with an uncle in Clare and gave about three and a half years there going to school. My uncle sent me down again and I gave a year here going to the National School. I came out of that at thirteen and learned shoemaking then.

Interviewer: Did you like school?

Patsy: I did in Clare, actually, and I liked Irish and the maths, and I used to like geography too, but don't ask me anything about them now!

Interviewer: Where did you go to school Seán?

Seán: I went to school here in Abbeyfeale but I hated it, I really hated it.

Interviewer: Why was that?

Seán: I really don't know. I was gone wild I suppose, wild during the War years.

Interviewer: Was that because you were living with your aunt and had a good time?

Seán: Oh no. During the war years, you see, I was going for my Catechism and the teacher met my father and he said, "Tom", Tom was my father's name, he said "Tom, you are rearing a young pagan." Sure, I didn't know God from the devil, and a young pagan I was. But that was my education and I left it before I was thirteen but after, I used to have nightmares that I was still at school. I used to wake up in a sweat because I thought I was there and I was a happy man in the morning when I realised that I didn't have to go anymore. That's how much I hated it.

Interviewer: Had you hard teachers?

Seán: Some of them were nice but more of them were a bit... well, we won't go into that at all. I often got a bit of a hiding over the map on the wall. One day a teacher carried me up to the map and asked me about foreign countries. Sure, what did I know about foreign countries? I got slashed across the legs for it anyway. There were more of them nice though. So when I left then I came to shoemaking, as I was all my life watching the shoemakers.

Interviewer: Was your father a shoemaker?

Seán: My father was a shoemaker, his two brothers were shoemakers and their father before them was a shoemaker and so was my father's uncle, Tom Ryan. They were living in Main Street across from the post office. Tom Ryan had fourteen men working for him, as well as his brother. Tom had only one son and he died at twenty-one under an operation. His brother then was married to one of the Meade's, our grandmother, so that's where the family came in. I was always looking at the shoemaking even when we were small and we saw great shoemakers. Do you want the names of shoemakers?

Interviewer: Yes, indeed.

Seán: I am only going back to my generation now, the crowd that I knew. You had Maurice Callaghan, Timmy Brouder, Curtin and Mick Wall. Mick Wall was a shoemaker with Mick Collins of Colbert's Terrace. Patsy Collins' father was a shoemaker, Mick Shannon, Larry (Tadhg Lar) Connors, Frank Noonan was a shoemaker and there were other ones in between then. I don't know were they shoemakers or repairers. There was a great character out there,he is probably in the books, Tommy Meehan.

Interviewer: So there were a lot of apprentices here in your fathers' time?

Seán: There were no apprentices when we were growing up because the shoemaking was going down but they had them before us all right. In old Tom Ryan's shop there used to be journeymen, who moved from town to town, but would come in and would make shoes while they were on the road. One great shoemaker was Fitz the shoemaker, as they used to call him.

Seán: Another one of them stayed below with my uncle Jackie Ryan and would make the shoes below there. There was a lot of those men very talented. Maurice Callaghan and more of them then went into making a lighter shoe. We had an uncle, Dan, who was a genius at this soled shoes, like priests' Sunday shoes you'd see, but the most of it was gone when we were coming up, it was dying out then. We made the last two pairs of shoes, myself and Patsy, in 1962.

Patsy: It was going down during the War years, when you couldn't get the stuff, though some managed to get it all right.

Seán: The Ryans had a good business going but you could only get a certain quota of material. It was like the ration cards in that way.

Patsy: We mentioned a man there, Mick Collins, he specialised in ladies shoes, or ladies boots, we could call them, and they were made entirely of leather.

Seán: First of all you had to cut out the shoe from big sheets of leather, or hides they were. You would get another piece then, insole leather, which was lighter and the uppers would be made of a soft kip.

Interviewer: Where was that sourced?

Seán: I really don't know, but the hides came from tanneries that time and our father used to get it from O'Callaghan's of Tralee. I don't know where the Ryan's got it before that but they were dealing with Carew's in Limerick as well so it was coming fom O'Callaghan's, Carew's, and we got leather one time from Cork.

Patsy: The first Ryan's, going back to our grandfathers' time, used to cut out the uppers from different hides and then they would sew it up. In our generation then, we used to get the uppers cut out and all from Long's in

Dublin. After they came down, all we had to do was to machine stitch them, which was fine, but it wasn't good enough for the hand made shoes, and we had to sew the quarters by hand with wax thread.

Seán: Next, you would have to wet all the leather to soften it for a couple of days because you couldn't work it and it was too hard. You could work the insole leather all right, but the sole leather would have to be softened. The one thing about it was that there was a great smell off of that leather, a terrible stink, and the funny thing was that the farmers used to come in looking for it.

Interviewer: There was a cure in it?

Seán: They said there was for warts in horses and for the warble fly on the cows, but that fly had an awful effect on the leather.

Patsy: When we used to get the hides, you'd see a small little red or black mark from the fly on the leather and we would have to go around that because if we didn't, it would soak up all the water in Ireland. They got some chemicals for it after but they hadn't them at the time.

Seán: The best upper of all time was kip. There was another upper that was known as split, but you might as well be trying to work wood than work that. You'd then have to pull the upper to shape and then leave it dry. We'd come on then with our knife and we'd shape it for the shoe. The next thing was then we'd get the uppers and we'd stitch the quarter. Then the upper was embellished from inside and stiffeners were put at the back to keep them up. There was no glue like you have today to hold them but what we were able to do was we'd get flour and mix it with water and that would make a paste. You would put it in then and when it hardened it held in place.

The upper was put in then and you would leave up the heel behind and last it from that part in the toe, pulling the upper around. The loose leather was stripped then with your inch tack. A thread was made then, seven or nine inches long, and with a sewing awl, you would catch the upper and the insole with basic stitches all along. You were nearly home and dry then and all you had to do was fill in the centre with a bit of insole leather and that was the foundation of a shoe. Another sole was put over that, known as a slip, and the slip was pegged and then you might put in a bit of a thing, what do you call it?

Patsy: A stiffener.

Seán: A stiffener at the back of it there and then there was a tip put on them.

Patsy: You would have hobnails on the second sole, and the tip nail then was in the heel.

Seán: Before you did that you had to rub the bone to the shank, I don't know was it a dog's bone or a cow's bone, but it would bring up a gold colour at the back of the shank. We used to make glass knives out of butts of saws and you would plane it all the way to give it a good face and when it was finished you would nail it then with a blue square nail.

Interviewer: Could you get any colour you wanted in the leather?

Seán: The leather was all the same for the upper and it was either black or brown.

Patsy: Carew's were the wholesalers and they used to stock an awful lot of leather. Reps would be coming around in vans and you could buy all the stuff for the boots, the shoes and all the supplies outside at the door from them. This was after the War now, as we couldn't do a bit during it. Our father went to work for Timmy Brouder when we were young and that is why I was working for him.

Interviewer: Was it there you learned your trade?

Patsy: I learned it here at Ryan's but I was working for him because I was getting money there, though it wasn't much, although seven and six was a bit that time.

Interviewer: Was that a week's wages or a day's wages?

Patsy: No, that was for every pair of boots.

Interviewer: Seven and six for a pair of boots, and what would they sell them for then?

Patsy: I don't know, I wouldn't be sure.

Seán: First of all they were two pounds and five shillings and then they went up then to two pounds and ten shillings, an awful fist of money. I remember years after I went to Limerick and I went into a shoe repairer and we were talking about prices. When I said I was getting three and six for a pair of heels he told me I was working for the other world! I thought it was a great price.

Patsy: I'll tell you one thing, the biggest insult you can give a shoemaker is to call him a cobbler, they hate it. They are two different trades. There were benchmen as well and a bootmaker can be a cobbler and bootmaker, but a cobbler can't be a bootmaker and that's the difference.

Interviewer: Was it all leather that was used in the shoes and was the leather of better that time than later on?

Seán: It was all leather that time and was of great quality of course but it was hard to work it, even when making the light shoes.

Patsy: I'll tell you a great one about a man that used to come in here. I'll always remember as a young lad that time my father would make a pair of boots, or we would make a pair of boots ourselves, for the farmer, or whoever it would be, and two years those boot would hold him, no doubt about it, and he inside in drains and everything. This fellow came in one day and he said to Tom, "Tom, these boots weren't so good at all as I only have them a year and a half." And this was the job I got, take off the nails, take off the sole, take off the insole, insole them again, sole them again, nail them and tip them. That alone would usually come for about ten shillings and they were practically new boots. All because they didn't last the full two years for him!

Interviewer: What would have been a busy day in the shop for selling shoes?

Seán: The November fair when the people would be coming in from all over. Outside in the shop there would be wires and rows of shoes hanging off of them. They would be making them throughout the year for the fair because the winter was coming on too.

Patsy: But they would be buying them through the year too. Some farmers would come in, especially from the Rock' and Meelin, and would pay you for that boot months before you had it made. You would take their name and they would pay you for the boot and you would have it ready for them when they wanted it. That goes to show you how very honest they were.

Interviewer: How long did your apprenticeship take?

Patsy: It took me four years but we were looking at it all our lives. It was a special craft too, you see, and the most of it was in the eye.

Seán: Yes, all in the eye. If you had a good eye and good hands you were grand.

Patsy: Just like watching the girls!

Seán: I don't know about you and watching girls, but I was only watching the shoes!

September 1933 sees the formation of Fine Gael, following an amalgamation of Cumann na nGaegheal, Centre Party and the National Guard (The Blueshirts). Eoin O'Duffy was its first leader.

The Dubliners, one of Irelands longest surviving and best loved folk groups, forms in 1962.

Sean O'Connell - Harness making

I was born here in this house here on Upper Maiden Street, Newcastle West. There was seven in the family, five boys and two girls. Today, there are two of the boys in the States and my sister in Louisiana is a nun. Another of my brothers is a Christian Brother who was teaching in Nenagh but is retired now.

My father was a harness maker and it was from him that I learned the trade. My mother died when we were young, when I was only about fourteen and the youngest. I had no notion of going into the trade, but before she died, she asked me that if anything happened her, would I go into the trade with my father. So I did and stayed on at it until 1983.

It was a long service and it started to go down at one time. I said to myself that I had better do something before it goes down altogether. So I went to Aughinish and got a job there in the catering side and was there for about nine years and loved it. It was a big difference from harness making but when I was working with my father, we depended on people coming in and out to us.

We did a big trade at the time and we also made a lot of hurling balls as well, to supplement the harness making. We got into making the balls because my father was a great G.A.A. man himself and went to all the matches. So we worked long hours, maybe between nine and eleven hours a day, and he used to always say, "Well, you won't get us in the morning but you will get us at night" because we often worked very late hours, anything up to eleven or twelve at night.

There were three other harness makers in Newcastle at the time; Nash's and Kennedy's and the O' Dwyer's in Church Street, and then Luddy came on after him.

The centre of the hurling ball was made from cork and the leather on the outside we imported from Edinburgh in Scotland. It was imported especially from the tanners there as they usen't manufacture that type of leather at all in Ireland. The harness leather was made in Callaghan's of Limerick at the tanneries there. But we supplied all the local clubs with the sliothars and we did a good trade with Elvery's of Dublin and Cork. They were wholesalers and supplied many the Christian Brothers schools as well.

We made harnesses for the cart horse and for the driving horse but all that went out with the coming in of the motor car. My father specialised in making horses' collars and sent a lot of them to other harness makers that weren't able to make the collar. We didn't do much in the way of saddles as that was a different side of the trade, saddlery, but we repaired them all right.

My father often went back to Kerry to get the rye reed for making the collars, as it was grown back there. There wasn't much rye reed sown around here, just the wheaten straw but he used both. The collars were turned out and the straw put into the main body but there was a lining as well on the outside that was stuffed with hair. Before we got a machine for stitching the rims, we used to sew them by hand. On the machine, it took maybe an hour whereas it would take maybe two and a half to three hours to do it by hand and that was a big difference. Hemp was used for stitching the leather and when it was waxed, six threads were rolled together into a wax cord and you could work it then with one or two needles.

Four years was usually how long it took to serve your time but you could be learning something new every day after that. My father was the first member of the family to go into harness making. He came from Ashford and was only fourteen years old when he came to Newcastle West to serve his time. He went into Limerick after his four years and after that he went to Cork City and worked in a place on Patrick Street where he was full time making collars.

It was around the eighties that things got quiet. There was a big business up to then and I was on my own since my father died in 1967. It was going down then with the coming of the tractors. They were now taking the milk to the creamery, whereas the horse and car was taking it before that. They started taking the bulk tank with the motor car first and then the tractor came on and the trailer.

That was that, so I went to Aughinish and spent nine good years there. I washed the pots and the pans and helped the chef then. It was a big change but I liked it. I was up in the morning at half past seven and coming along the road to be in for half eight and I often did a lot of overtime there. I often worked the Saturday and Sunday and I was well used to the long hours at home, so the long hours didn't mean anything to me when I went to Aughinish.

In my younger days, I used to go to the bog and spend a week out there in Toureennagreana with my cousin John P.O'Connell. He, his brothers and I would go out to the bog there at nine o'clock in the morning and be there until six or seven in the evening. I'd work away with them and for my efforts they would give me a load of turf. There was a big business in the turf cutting there, and it was all by hand and the sleán at that time, but now the machine cuts it. You had coal as well but we couldn't get it during the war, as it wasn't coming in from England, so it was all turf.

There was some good characters here in Newcastle West always. You had a fellow by the name of John Joe Houlihan below at the end of Maiden street who's people were coopers, Atty McCarthy and Rathar McCarthy. Then of the younger crowd you had Mike O'Brien who came from Knockane and Tom Houlihan who was another cooper. They were special and they'd have their few drinks in the pub and meet the other characters there and bring out all the stories from there but I'd forget them all now as my memory is fading out.

There was a lot of other trades here on Maiden Street. There were many shoemakers in town and I remember one man across the road, about sixty five years ago, and his name was Willie Hartnett. He sold out his place, got married and bought a farm of land over in Knockaderry. There were the Hartes of Maiden Street, Mikey Hayes, who's son now is taking it on and also Pat Mackessy and Mick O'Sullivan up on Church Street. There was the Houlihans and another cooper by the name of Davie Keating, over in St. Ita's terrace, and also Tom O'Sullivan who was a tinsmith. They are all dead now and it's only myself I'd say that's left.

There were bakers here too, like the Murphys, the Fitzgeralds, and the Nashes. There were tailors like the O'Connor's here on Maiden Street, Jim O' Donnell on South Quay and his son Oliver after him and a young lad down on North Quay by the name of Lacy but I don't think there is a tailor left in town today. I went to school with a chap by the name of Christy Reidy who was a carpenter and worked in Feenagh at coffin making. His son now is at that business.

I don't train any apprentices or anything now. You wouldn't get any young lads to go into the trades as there would be nothing there for them. There is a good bit to be done in the saddlery business but I don't know of any people that are at it, maybe there is someone in Limerick, but there is another harness maker up in William Street, a namesake of mine, Willie O'Connell, and he is doing fairly well there, making belts, dog collars and leads and things like that.

I get up every day, read the paper and I go for a walk up the Demesne along a couple of miles of lovely paths. I still love to meet people and can go up there and meet the boys. The town has become very quiet and there was a time here on Maiden Street that you wouldn't see a motor car all but the place would be full of donkeys, ponies and horses and it was very busy indeed.

Old stitching machine used by Sean O'Connell

1967: Fees are abolished in most secondary schools in the Republic.

1983: Terrorist explosion kills two hundred and thirty-seven U.S. Marines in Beirut.

Tom Begley

My name is Tom Begley of Bridge Street, Abbeyfeale and I was born in the town in 1928. I had two brothers and two sisters but my two sisters have passed away now. My parents lived and worked in Abbeyfeale. It was hard to rear a family that time because there was no money around.

I went to school in Abbeyfeale but I never liked it and I left at sixteen.

My father and my uncle were black-smiths and when I left school, I went into apprenticeship with my uncle and that was my first job. I learned the trade from him. I'd put on six sets of shoes on the horses in a day. There was a lot of business in the horse trade that time. The tools we used were hammer and pinchers and all the tools were made by us, made out of iron. Iron was plentiful then, but during the War, there was little coal to fire it. We got the coal from Cork through a permit, so many hundredweight in the month, and so on. When iron went scarce, we would have to make the shoes out of old shoes by putting four old shoes together and making one new one. When the welder came out in 1943 it made things very easy for the blacksmith.

The forge was outside on the street but they moved it back into this work-shop then when the road was made wider, there must have been no traffic or nothing that time.

There was said to be a cure in forge water and people that had warts would come in there and they'd dip the warts in the water in the trough to see if they could get rid of them.

We'd never work Holy days but we'd never take holidays either, and often you'd get no bed for May, June and July except for Saturday and Sunday nights. You'd never go to bed Monday, Tuesday, Wednesday, Thursday and Friday, as you'd be fixing mowing machines and wheels.

All the news would be trashed out sitting there from ten o'clock in the morning until six in the evening.

To put the bands on the wheels you'd put fourteen wheels into the yard and you'd put three rails of turf around the fourteen bands and redden them. Then I'd bring them in here to the workshop and put them up on the stand and cut and make the band an inch and a half smaller than the wheel and weld it in the fire, and go out then and put it down around the timber wheel and throw the water down on top of it to cool it down. There would be water everywhere but you'd have to use the water quick before the timber of the wheel went on fire. There were two days in the week for shoeing the wheels, Friday and Saturday. It was a big job and was always done on Saturday mornings at about five o'clock before the sun would come out, in the cool of the early morning.

The horses would be shod every day. The wet day was a fright though, and they'd come in after the harvest and there would be thirty or forty horses in the yard.

When the tractor came in then we were finished, as there were no more horses being used on the farm. That changed the work a lot, as there would be no more bands or horseshoes falling off. Putting rubber wheels on the common cars was a great plan.

I never played any sport. I had no interest, especially when you would have your day's work done, and after shoeing six or seven horses you wouldn't have much time for entertainment. We had the first or second television in town and we had the second motor car in town in 1935 or '36. It was the Model T Ford.

There was a holy well in Dromtrasna called St. Ita's and there would be a big crowd going up there in the month of May. St. Ita's day is the 15th January and there would be a big crowd going to Killeedy, as she is the patron saint of that village.

The Emergency years were hard and tea and sugar was rationed, as was iron, and worse again, the coal was rationed. As I said, we were making old shoes out of scrap and everything. There were people that couldn't pay too and it was an awful time. They had no money and you'd get nothing out of them but you'd still have to buy the coal and the iron to keep going.

1928: The first Forestry Act of Saorstat Eireain was introduced in 1928.

*Gay Byrne, who would become the host of the worlds longest running live talk show ever, was born in **1934**.*

Tom McCarthy

I am Tom McCarthy of Caherhayes, Co. Limerick. I was born in Cappafaudeen in County Cork with three brothers and three sisters. My mother was at home, doing the housework all the time and my father was caretaking in land, that's what I'd call it anyway. We had sixteen cows at the time when we came to Meenkilly and I was around three years of age. We had only the cows and a horse and car, and the land would not grow flax, oats or barley because it was all mountain and the meadows that were there were needed for hay for the cows.

I went to Meenkilly School and I liked it. We walked it to school through the fields in summer but we would have to go the road in the winter. There was a glen you couldn't cross in the wintertime with the floods, so you would have to go the road about two miles and a half out of the way. There were three teachers there; Mrs. Mary O'Connor from Caherhayes, Johnny Harnett from Springmount and the third teacher there was Andrew Downey and he was from Ballinasloe.

The new school was built either in 1915 or in 1916. We did a good bit of Irish and English but there were no religion classes at that stage. We had singing two evenings a week for which we used to go up to the top room to sing for about a half an hour. I left school at fourteen years of age and nearly all my friends finished that time too, and after that they all went out working, to what we used to call "out in service".

My first job was in Abbeyfeale, at Tim Warren's shop. He used to have a little garden out at the back where he would have potatoes, parsnips, carrots and onions, but he was a wholesaler in tea and sugar and cigarettes and everything. He would have me in weighing out pounds of sugar and pounds of tea. I would also be cleaning all the brass knobs in the doors and cleaning inside around the shop.

I started there at fourteen years of age, right after leaving school. I would be up there in the morning about seven o' clock and at finishing time at six o' clock, the gate would be closed. He had a big yard there at the time when the fairs used to be in Abbeyfeale. There were no cars around then and the buyers used to come up from Newcastle West on a horse and trap and often park in the yard. He had a loft over the yard where he used to keep the tea and sugar and more of the yard was open and I would have to take the cushions out of the traps and anything else that they would have inside in it, like rugs, and I would put them into a shed until they would come up again in the evening. I was getting eleven pounds a month from him and I often made three or four pounds inside in the yard for minding the belongings of people.

He had a big black car, I don't know what was the make of it, that had curtains in the windows of it. He used to go down to Puck Fair with it and once, we went down to Foynes to see the seaplanes coming in there in it. There were curtains in the window of the car and you could pull them across if you wanted to sleep there. A Cork man he was himself and he always went there for a week with his wife and I would go in every morning just open the yard.

I went into him when I started with a short pants, and after the first year I gave him, at Easter, he went down the town and he brought up two suits of clothes from Dan Sullivan's for me to pick one out. He brought me up a suit, a shirt, jumper, tie, socks and shoes and it was he that put the long pants on me. The following Easter he did the very same thing again and I got another suit from him.

I went out then to Muirisheen Daly outside in Caherhayes and I gave two years with him. I put down a good time there because he was a fine sober man and there was no hurry in the world in him. Myself and his wife Cathy would milk the cows and then I would go to the creamery with an ass and car. When I came home, we would be jobbing around the yard and in the summer we would be in the meadow saving the hay. He would have the oats and potatoes and all then in the autumn. I left after two years with him.

Jack Thomasheen O'Connell from Meenkilly was my next stop and I gave a year there and I left that and I gave a year to Kate O'Keeffe above in Knockadereen, the Hill. I went down to Maurice O'Connor in Grogeen and gave eleven years hard work there between going and coming. There was a man next door, Donal Pat O'Connor, Donaleen Pats we used to call him, and he would be always be whistling every morning going down across the house. The very minute Katie, Maurice's wife, would hear him, she would give a roar and I would have to get up then.

I was sleeping in a press bed inside in the kitchen as they had only the one room. There was no bolt on the door or anything, only a catch, and the last one in at night had to throw a bag of turf up against it to keep it closed. In the mornings, she would call me and I would jump out of the bed, catch the tongs, and rattle them to let on that I was up. When I did get up, I put down the fire and put down the kettle and I would go out for the cows to bring them in. There were eleven cows there and I often had three or four of them milked before she came out to me.

I would go on then and go for the cows and that took about ten minutes or a quarter of an hour, according to where they were, and I would milk eight of them cows out of the eleven. I would have to go over then, over the field, to Danny Mike Noble's and cut a barth of rye in the hail, rain or storm. You would have to have it fresh for them and I would put that into a rope, bring it up on my back, and put it in to them. The horses, which he also had, ate a couple of stone of oats with the rye.

There was an old shed outside in the yard and I would be in it with a butchers knife and a Sacred Heart lamp cutting turnips and mangles for the cows in the morning to feed them. There was no stopping time, and I used to work there from once the spring work would start until the potatoes were dug, from around six o' clock in the morning until nine or ten o'clock at night. They were good times, and it was a pound a month I was getting.

The fairs were good and there were stands and everything there that time. I remember a lad there and he would be lying up on a big ring made with nails and he would lie onto the nails with his two hands out. When he stood up all you could see were the marks of the nails.

There was a man there this day and he had a cow he was selling. Anyway, he wanted twelve pounds for the cow and this man, Con Wren, said he would give him ten. After a long time bargaining the man put up the two hands to Con and, Con said, "I'll give you that", thinking the man had settled for ten pounds.

Later on, Con was paying your man and he was giving him the ten pounds. "No," said the man, "it was twelve pounds." "By God, 'twas not," says Con "wasn't I there today when you said so!" "You were," he said and he put up his two hands. "Count them," says he. He had six fingers in each hand! Con got an awful land and he had to give him the twelve pounds.

I went over to England on the beet on the first of September 1948 and I came home in March 1949. I married on the first of September 1949 and I went on the beet to England again three weeks after marrying. It was hard work. I wasn't ever in England for St. Patrick's day. Oh, you would of course be left wear emblems, no bother in the world. They wore them there from the start when they were going over, and when St. Patrick's day would come, work or not, they would take off that day and wear the shamrock

When the beet started at that stage there was an awful pile of Irish people going over, winter after winter, for eight or nine years, but some bought farms of land out of it. We were staying in hostels. It was fifteen pounds a week for our bed and grub but you could see it was all horsemeat you were getting. You could see the blood in it and it wouldn't be half cooked. Some of the boys would catch the plate and throw it up to your man inside the counter and ask him where the hoof of the horse was! They would give you a pack then going out to work, but you couldn't eat it and you would have to buy buns or biscuits or a few sandwiches. It was like money gone for nothing for your grub there because you couldn't eat it.

It was all eight-hour shifts we worked and you would give a fortnight in days and then a fortnight in nights. It was constant going like that there from September until March. When you would be going over then, you would have to go up to Dublin, about five hours on the train from Abbeyfeale, and then on to Liverpool, another eleven hours on the water.

When you would go up to Dublin, they would give you a big examination to see if you were fit. If your clothes had what they used to call fleas and boodies and things like that, they would have to would go through some kind of a machine with disinfectant and the smell that used to be out of them! I knew a few of the boys that had their clothes sent through and it was something desperate the smell that was out of them after they came back.

I never played many games when I was young, but often there would be eight or nine of us and we would go over into Danny Mike Noble's field and we would be hurling there. There would be handles of brushes or the handle of a pickaxe or something used as there would be no such thing as hurleys, when we belted the ball around the place. I never was interested in matches though. I am now, but I'd rather watch them on the television than to go to any match up in Cork or Dublin. I would go to see the local teams all right, as they would be good matches too.

The people would go roving from house to house that time, to see your neighbours and go in to talk to them. There were raffles in the wintertime and often dancing and music and all that. People from around the place, with the fiddle and accordion, would provide the music. We often travelled five and six miles to raffles. They were very popular, but the card play was a different thing altogether. The card play was only a gamble and might only hold until two or three o' clock in the morning but in the raffle, you would get bread and tea and that would hold out for the full night. There would be a batch of us together walking home and we often travelled in a foot of snow and not a drop of drink in us.

On the Wren nights, they would go out and they would collect the money for the wren and you would join in to help them out if they didn't have enough and I went on the "wran" several times over the years. Jack Lane, from Kilkinlea, used to play for us that time. He was a great player, but if you brought anyone into the house while he was playing that night, he would nearly get up and walk out. He would hold at it all night but he didn't want anyone else to come and play with him. We had him over at the cottage for several winters and a huge crowd altogether would gather, often with a couple of barrels of porter drank, no bother to them.

I used to love the Christmas, coming home out of service and it would be seven or eight o'clock in the evening before you would be left go. You would have to do the last job for them on Christmas Eve. If you promised you would go back to them the following year you would get a half a crown, which was a good bit of money that time, and if you weren't going to them then you would get nothing, not a ha'penny, from them. At Christmas, you would have the big round currant loaf and the currant bread as well. You wouldn't see it at all during the year, and then you might have maybe a bit of beef or a bit of mutton or something, but more of them then would buy the goose. It was more the goose that time than the turkey and they would boil the goose and get the soup and meat off it. It used to be beautiful.

If you were expecting Santa, you'd get up in the morning and there might be a sweet and maybe a biscuit inside in your sock and you would be delighted. Candles would be lighting all the time, usually two candles in the kitchen that they wouldn't carry with them in the rooms like but that they would leave in the kitchen. Not just anyone could light them, most of the time it was the father or the mother that would light them. Often they would get a turnip, make a hole in it and put the candle standing into it. Then they would place it up in the window inside or put them up on the table and they would be lighting there all night. On Christmas morning, everyone in the house would go to Mass. We would generally go to the first mass because we would be up already for Santa.

I used to hear about the "Barna Spirit" when I was young, that she used to go into the meadows and knock the cocks of hay. I heard a person saying one time, she went into a car to two people, a husband and wife, but the man had a blackthorn stick and she went away. They said that it was the blackthorn stick that saved them, whatever was in it, and she could not go near them with it. There are lots of fairy forts around all right, and there was one in a field where we were staying in Meenkilly that I used to be in dread of my life of. There was a kiln along side it and no one went near it at all. They wouldn't even cut the hay around it or anything off of it, but they would let the cows into it and let them eat away. It is gone for years now.

I didn't hear much about the 1916 Rising. I used to hear them talking about the time of the Troubles with the Free Staters, and Gerry "The Bomber" Foley, as they used to call him. He used to go down to Danny O'Donnell's kiln and the Free Staters would be below around the square and he would blaze out from behind the kiln and down to them with a gun, putting them running in all directions. They would come out to the house looking for him and he had a brother, Frank, that was much like him and they often carried him away with them, but left him go again. I never knew him but I saw photos of him all right. He was very young, only seventeen or eighteen years. He was shot after, over in Meenahala at Collin's. He stayed there that night and someone, I suppose, gave some information that he was there. The woman of the house called him that morning when she saw the soldiers coming but he hadn't time enough to escape. He ran into an outside cabin and the first soldier that went in after him, a Foley man, who was a first cousin of his, they said, was shot dead. He jumped out over him, wounded another lad and he ran. It was up against the hill he went but if he had went down with the fall of ground, they wouldn't have got him at all because the bullets would be going out over his head, but he got stuck in a couple rows of wire there and they shot him. I often heard them saying that he wasn't killed outright but that his guts were hanging out and they carried him in below to the barrack. There was someone there that wanted to shoot him but the Corporal there, I don't know his name, said no. He said that if there were two more like him, they would free Ireland. Foley was in hospital for a long time after that and then he went over to America and he never came back. He married a girl from Limerick when he went over there, as far as I know. And that was *Gerry Foley, the boy from the Hill.*

I remember the rations, the tea and the sugar, and you would get it on the black market. The funny part about it is that if you could pay for it, you would get all you wanted of it if you knew where to get it. That time it was cocoa and coffee people were drinking but I'd drink milk before I would drink them. We had that when we were over in the beet as well and the cigarettes and all were next impossible to get. There were a couple of them with me when we were in the beet that weren't smoking at all. I was smoking and I would get tickets for so many packages of fags, and I was able to get enough of them between my own and their tickets. They would do me for the week and only for that I don't know what I would have done!

The children of today have a great life now. I met my wife, Maureen, below in Abbeyfeale Hill and we were only going together about eight or nine months when we got married. She was nineteen years old and I was twenty-three. We had twelve children and there was no bathrooms or toilets that time in the cottage and only the two rooms. If a couple had that family now it's a hospital they would want to put them into. You wouldn't get them to go into a cottage now in a fit!

1926: A general strike in Britain brings the nation's activities to a standstill.

1949: Council of Europe established. Ireland and Britain are amongst founding members.